EXPLAINING
THE UNEXPLAINABLE

Kathleen Miller

The Book Guild Ltd.
Sussex, England

The Book Guild Ltd.
25 High Street,
Lewes, Sussex.

First published 1993
© Kathleen Miller 1993
Set in Baskerville
Typesetting by Southern Reproductions (Sussex)
East Grinstead, Sussex.
Printed in Great Britain by
Antony Rowe Ltd.
Chippenham, Wiltshire.

A catalogue record for this book is
available from the British Library

ISBN 0 86332 777 X

I would like to dedicate this book to those who gave great encouragement and assistance in their own way. These being:
'Cousin Ivy'
Jane Pepper and her husband Ron Pepper
Mary Ingham, and also of course Guy Lyon Playfair for the introduction he so kindly wrote.

PREFACE

Although we have helped Kathleen Miller put this book together, the essential words and experiences are those of the author. Our function has been purely that of practical assistance with typing and minor revisions.

What you have before you is a genuine and verifiable account of an ordinary life lived by someone whose experiences, perceptions and understandings are extraordinary. Over four months we witnessed the writing of this book by someone who had had little formal education and whose life style is modest and unpretentious. We have been able to check the truth of the events described, events which are all the more impressive because they are rooted in everyday life.

During these months we have ourselves undergone a change of attitude towards many aspects of the unexplained and can see now how the author's findings offer a coherent and realistic analysis. The proof of the theory lies in its application to the large number of events, often apparently mundane but connected, which we all experience but which may all too easily be brushed off as coincidental or just plain oddities.

Once you have yourself tested Kathleen Miller's theory and techniques and have seen them to be self-evidently true, then you will find you have a clearer understanding of many aspects of your life. You may well also discover you have talents of which you were perhaps totally unaware.

There are some who will find what is written to be difficult to accept. The author challenges the validity of spiritualism, faith healing, fortune telling and clairvoyance, as well as explaining hauntings, apparitions, poltergeist activity and religious miracles. The explanation is simple, the implications enormous. These findings, which came from within the author and are not based on any kind of academic theorising but real life experience, place upon us all a heavy responsibility – that we, ourselves, are basically and irrevocably responsible for everything that happens to us and to those around us.

Read on – and think carefully,

Ron and Jane Pepper

INTRODUCTION

At an early age, the author of this unusual and remarkable book discovered that she could do things others apparently could not. If she wished strongly enough for something, she would almost immediately get it. She would know when a friend or relative was going to die. She could 'recall' events that had not yet taken place. Later in life she found that she could ease people's aches and pains by just placing her hands on the affected part of the body. She also developed an extraordinary ability to make coincidences happen. For instance, if she urgently needed a certain sum of money, she would go to her club and win the precise amount. She could, and still can, influence events around her merely by taking the decision to do so.

In search of an explanation for her strange powers, she has turned neither to scientists nor to spirit guides for help. She has tackled the problem herself, and in her opinion she has solved it. She attributes all of her unusual talents to the powers of her own mind and its ability to form 'mind-chains' that in turn influence the thoughts and actions of others. These are forged by nothing other than her own will, or as she prefers to put it, by her precise instructions to her subconscious mind. Thus her wishes come true as the minds of others find themselves obeying them.

In earlier times we treated our unusually gifted children with respect. We trained them to become shamans – people whose extended senses qualified them for the job of intermediary between our world and that of the gods or spirits, a job that practically all societies have considered both useful and necessary. Nowadays, however, with our world in the safe hands of politicians and scientists, we have no place for such people, and we do our best to ignore or suppress their

9

claimed abilities. We explain them away with such labels as 'secondary personality', 'exteriorised consciousness' or simply 'hallucination'. And, of course, that old favourite 'coincidence', which explains everything. Whatever the real nature or these abilities, we would rather not know. If we were to know, the authority of the arbiters of our society would be undermined. Such an attitude may make us feel safer, but it is no help at all to the individuals concerned.

Physically gifted children still run the risk of being labelled mentally abnormal. They may be forced to suppress their vivid imaginations, or told that such gifts as clairvoyance and telepathy are manifestations of the powers of the devil. The lucky ones may grown up to become 'mediums' and earn a respectable living by providing their services for seekers of contacts with other worlds and dimensions. Even so, they face condemnation as 'frauds', and the more successful among them will be debunked in the Sunday papers, or at best regarded as harmless but deluded eccentrics.

All such an attitude achieves is to postpone investigation into something that has a right to be investigated: the human mind.

The Society for Psychical Research was founded in 1882 to explore the border areas of human personality, yet it was to be more than a century before our first university department was set up for the purpose of examining the various fields that we have lumped together under the label of parapsychology. (This came about, it must be remembered, not on the initiative of any scientist or politician, but on that of the writer Arthur Koestler, after whom the new chair at the University of Edinburgh is named).

It is to be hoped that books such as this will find their way into the syllabus of this pioneering department. If we are to study the workings of unusual minds, it helps if we have a lucid account written by the owner of such a mind, which is precisely what we have here. It contains a number of details that will interest parapsychologists, such as the author's observation that she uses her 'right brain' in order to get what she wants, or the fact that as a young baby she suffered a blow on her head. It is now known that our two brain halves operate in quite different ways, and also that many unusually gifted people have had their gifts apparently awakened by blows to the head. Edgar Cayce, the 'sleeping clairvoyant' was struck by a baseball bat; the Dutchman Peter Hurkos fell off a ladder; the Brazilian automatic writer Chico Xavier was battered as a young child. Such accidents or acts of violence seem to have stimulated the brains of the victim to develop unexpectedly rather than to suffer any kind of damage or limitation.

Alfred Russell Wallace, one of the originators of the theory of natural selection, devoted a chapter of one of his books to the 'residual phenomena' that he felt could not be explained by the theory for which he and Darwin are known. One was the fact that primitive man had a brain that was much larger than it needed to be. As he put it, 'natural selection would only have endowed savage man with a brain a little superior to that of an ape, whereas he actually possesses one very little inferior to that of a philosopher'. It was, he said, as if 'a superior intelligence has guided the development of man in a definite direction, and for a special purpose'. Wallace also argued that since it was known that some kind of force or energy originated in the human mind, 'it does not seem an improbable conclusion that all force may be will-force'.

Our brains remain largely unused and undeveloped. Why has nature provided us with something we apparently do not need, and something we definitely do not fully employ? Could it not be that the so-called psychic abilities (telepathy, clairvoyance, precognition) are not vestiges of primitive skills, as has been suggested, but facilities that await development?

If so, this book offers us a glimpse of things to come. Its author's matter-of-fact approach makes it more persuasive than many a learned philosophical discourse on the nature of man. She has learned to live with her unusually developed mind, and she has also learned not to misuse it. Her refusal to seek refuge in any kind of occult belief system commands our respect, as does her honest and straightforward account of a most unusual life.

Guy Lyon Playfair

11

FOREWORD

This is an entirely true account of the very strange life I have led which has involved many aspects of phenomena that various people have experienced throughout the ages with no apparent explanation.

I am a very average kind of middle-aged woman with no connection whatsoever with spiritualism, or the occult of any description, yet I have the most amazing story to reveal.

I feel positive that the contents of this book will be of great interest to everyone alike, whether they be a believer or a non-believer in such claims, religious or an atheist.

My findings are based purely on my own experiences, all that came from within, and all that was finally revealed to me in 1984, and I sincerely believe them to be of great importance to mankind.

1

Although in the very early part of my childhood I felt I was different from other children, I had no proof that this was so. I was nine years old when it began to become apparent.

These were the war years and I lived in London throughout the blitz. All that was happening was frightening enough for any child, but there was something happening in my life which was even more disturbing. How was it I often knew something was going to happen several weeks before it took place? How was it I knew who was going to call on me before they actually knocked at my door? Why did I always hear something about the very person I could not stop thinking about? Why did people invariably mention an item I had been thinking about? And how was I able to get the things I wanted, just by desperately wishing for them?

These were the kind of questions I asked myself over and over again. I desperately wanted to confide in someone but I knew that no one would believe me, since it was only after these things had taken place that I would realize I had known beforehand, and anyone could claim or pretend that, after the event. Then came the day I was convinced I had killed my brother's friend with my strange powers.

Although there were public shelters near to our home, our family often stayed at home during the nightly bombing raids that took place. One night, there was an air raid going on at the time I decided to go to bed. As I lay there just one person dominated my thoughts and try as I might, I could not get him out of my mind. His name was Billy Short. Billy was my brother's friend, he was sixteen years old and worked in a transport garage. In fact, he was on night shift at the time I was thinking about him - or so I thought.

The all clear finally sounded and I drifted off to sleep. I

woke up about 8.30 am and could hear several members of my family talking to someone at the front door. I waited until the person had gone and went downstairs to ask what was the matter. My mother said it was a neighbour who had called to tell us that Billy Short had been killed in the air raid the previous night. He had taken shelter on his way to work and the shelter got a direct hit. Only his identity card had been found. The alarm inside me rose to a pitch and I was panic stricken by one thought. 'Now I have killed Billy.' I felt he would be alive if I had not thought about him the night before.

Because his body had not been found I refused to believe he was dead and thought that he had dropped his identity card as he passed the shelter. But why hadn't he come home? Perhaps he had run away. Then I remembered what had taken place two weeks before.

Billy, my brother and another friend of theirs were all coming up to seventeen. They each had a set of three photographs taken to share out between one another, so that when they were called up they would have something to recall their friendship. Two weeks before Billy was killed we were all together in a crowded public air raid shelter. Billy was sitting about three or four feet from where I sat but for some unknown reason I found myself studying him closely. Usually he was loud and boisterous, but on this occasion he seemed depressed. Suddenly he pulled his set of three photographs from his pocket and gave them to a woman sitting nearby. I heard him say to her, 'Take these, I won't be needing them.' I believe I knew at that moment that he was going to die, and sure enough he did. The trouble was, I was convinced that I had killed him. For weeks I refused to believe he was dead and spent hours and hours willing him to knock on our door. I even revisited his old haunts many times in the hope of finding him.

But to tell the full story I must begin at the beginning.

I was born in the East End of London during the late 1920s, at the time of the depression. I was the middle member of a large Roman Catholic family of English and Irish descent. Like many thousands of other people of those times we were to experience the true meaning of the word poverty. My father like so many others was unemployed, and luxuries of any kind did not exist in our lives. We were never sure if there would be even a slice of bread to be had once the very small amount of dole money had run out, but in spite of our needs we were raised to respect everyone and everything including the old furniture we had, which had been passed on by my grandmother, or purchased for next to nothing.

When people are in the same boat it becomes a way of life to help each other and share what little they have. Clothes were passed from one family to the next after first having been passed down in the family they came from. In spite of this, our parents were proud people and repaid in kind for anything they received. This pride and consideration was passed on to us children and we were raised to expect nothing from anyone without appreciation. Because of the various Christian teachings there was a feeling of niceness among all those that you came into contact with, each person respected the other's religion, and each lived by their own. My parents being staunch Roman Catholics abided by the teachings of their faith. So many children were conceived by my mother, but less than half survived to maturity.

My earliest recollections are of being two and a half. I can recall many events that took place at that sad time and how my mother and father reacted to all they were to endure. Although there were many of us in the family, we lived in just two rooms at the top of a three-storey house. The outside bricks were old and I would feel sad when I studied them. It was a strange sensation and I cannot really put into words what I felt. A few years ago I returned to my place of birth and when looking at those bricks again I experienced the same strange sensation. I can recall how I liked to creep away from my brothers and sisters to be alone to think. It was not easy to be alone in such cramped conditions but I would say to myself, 'We will creep into the bedroom and be alone!' I never knew who *we* were. I would look out of the cold bedroom window at the many dismal smoking chimneys and just think.

I cannot recall my actual thoughts at this time only the fact that to think was the purpose for which I had gone into the bedroom.

I recall so many events from my pre-school days and details of conversations which took place between my mother and

17

father during these times. I recall so clearly the day my father sat me on his knee while my sister stood beside the wooden chair he sat on. I was just two and a half years old and my sister had turned four years of age. My father said to us 'I want you to say goodbye to Beth because she is going away.' I asked where Beth was going as she was our baby sister. My father said that Beth was going to heaven. He went on to say how good it was in heaven, and how Beth would be very happy there. I pleaded with him to let me go with her and pointed out that her present was still on the mantelpiece. Someone had bought her a box that had a cellophane lid and contained a little silver eggcup and spoon. Inside the cup was a chocolate Easter egg wrapped in coloured paper. My father said he would leave the present on the mantelpiece and when he died he would take it and give it to Beth. He then carried me into the adjoining room where Beth was lying in a lovely white box in the middle of the room. The lid to the box had been stood up against the wall, over by the window. I was lowered over to kiss Beth and my sister also kissed her. We had been back in the other room for just a moment or so when two men entered the room. They were all in black and had high hats on with black ribbon hanging at the back. They went into the room where Beth lay and came out with the white box on their shoulders, and took her away. For many months Beth's present stood on the mantelpiece and I often wished I could take it to her.

My sister Winnie was now at the age to start school. So my mother, Winnie and I went to the school our elder brothers and sisters were already attending for my mother to see the headmistress. The only part of the conversation that I remember was when the headmistress said, 'I will allow the younger one to start school and take her off your hands.' I was still just three years of age but liked the idea of going to school.

I recall so vividly the day when I came home from school and stopped as I entered our living room, shocked with horror. My grandmother sat at the table and having opened Beth's present was eating the chocolate egg. She looked at my father and said, 'Do you know, John, after all this time this egg is still all right.'

I hated her for what she had done and although she did not

die until I was about eight years old, I never talked with her and got to know her as my brothers and sisters did. This event was to have a lasting effect on me. My father had a habit of making little egg cups with his silver tobacco paper and would pass them to whichever of us children were near him when finished. I would try to move away so that I did not get one, because I felt I could never destroy it as it was Beth's silver cup and I felt such terrible guilt when I finally had to throw it away. Throughout my life I also hated Christmas presents in boxes like Beth's present, and would keep them for years unopened. I had one such box, containing talcum powder, for seven years.

It was quite usual in those days for a youngster to start school at the age of three, as I did. This was mainly because mothers had other young children to cope with and were invariably pregnant again. I can remember so much about this early part of my life, but never any sunshine. The sun must have shone but it just never reached our hearts and all those gloomy old buildings would hide the brightest day, along with the hunger and despair written on our parents' faces. I remember so clearly the day I started school, where I sat, and even what I wore. I remember how my sister and I were dressed alike in identical thin summer dresses that had been given by a relative who had two daughters a little older than we were. I felt so cold.

We were taken with other children into a classroom in which children were seated at their desks. The older children of the group were given seats among these children, whilst the very few young ones like myself were taken to the back of the classroom and seated at smaller desks and chairs. I wanted so badly to go and sit with my sister. During the afternoon the very young ones like myself were allowed to lie on small canvas beds to have a sleep. The beds were unfolded and set out in rows. I used to love this because while lying there in a quite classroom I was able to think without any interruption from a brother or sister. I used to think about the things the other children had said at school and what they did, or even wonder why they said or did a certain thing and I knew inside me that I was different from them.

I remember one occasion clearly from this period. When the school broke up for holidays we children had to remove the boxes fitted under our school tables and bring them home to scrub out all the chalk and dirt and then take them back to school after the holidays. On this particular last day, when I was now almost four, we all left the school carrying our wooden boxes but once outside the school the group of children I was with, including an older sister of mine, put their boxes in the middle of the road and, laughing and shouting, proceeded to kick them along the road instead of carrying them. Not wanting to be left behind, I also put my box down and gave two little kicks. I felt so very foolish behaving this way that I picked my box up and walked home alone with the feeling that I did not belong with them and that what they were doing was so very childish. Another time. at about the age of five, whilst out with a small two year old, I felt very embarrassed when we met a teacher from our school and I thought 'What must she think of me being with a two year old?' Looking back I know now that I should not have felt as I did, but *why* did I feel so much older than I really was at that age?

It was not until I had learnt to read and write that religion was really taught at school. Once I had received these teachings I did not feel different any more. I suppose I now had something to occupy my mind, religious thought instead of my own.

The late 20s and early 30s were bad times for ordinary people, with no work for the men and so many mouths to feed. My mother also had the task of keeping us children quiet because of the family living below. We had no garden, so this must have been a nightmare. Then, when I was six and a half, the good news came that we were moving to the outskirts of London into a house with a front and back garden! Compared to the East End, it was like moving into the heart of the country and it was wonderful actually to be near parks and woodlands. We stayed in this house for a couple of years and were then moved into a larger one due to the size of our family.

My memories of that house, unlike the flat in the East End, are only of summer. I hardly remember a winter at all. I was now a very strong believer in the Catholic religion. I believed that God was everywhere and saw all we did, I believed in Heaven and Hell and was afraid to do anything wrong. I don't mean I never got into trouble with my parents or argued with

20

a brother or sister. But if I forgot to say my prayers in the morning I would say them to myself on the way to school, fearing what would happen otherwise.

Although at this time of my life I no longer felt different, I retained the habit of studying what other children did or said. I probably envied them as I was very shy and self-conscious of the clothes I wore. They were always secondhand and were invariably either too small or too large. Unlike the East End, where most people were unemployed and as badly off as we were, we now lived amongst people who had work. Because my father was still unemployed our family stood out, but we children were clean and respectful and seldom did any of us bring trouble to our home.

About a year or so after moving into the larger house, World War II broke out and whilst the majority of children were evacuated to safety, a few remained. We stayed behind and now, due to a lack of teachers and children, all the schools closed down. I was eleven years old and like others who were not evacuated I earned pocket money by shopping for neighbours or doing whatever they required. My father, along with others who had been without work for so long, now had full employment. Being away from school I realized religion was becoming less and less important to me. With all that was going on around us, there was so much more to talk about. And with so many disturbed nights due to air raids, queuing for food and all that the war and its horrors brought to our lives, no one could remain the same kind of person as before.

After a very bad air raid, when many bombs dropped close to our home, I stood and watched the chaos, the effect of a direct hit on two houses. I watched as they brought out the bodies. It was 8 am on a Saturday. Children in their pyjamas were running around crying. There were injured women dressed ready to go shopping, a mother, whose child had been brought out dead from the rubble, was screaming. I was twelve years old and could do nothing but stare at this dreadful scene. Then suddenly I felt anger such as I had never known. It was not the Germans I hated, it was the God I'd been so devoted to all my life. At last I left to go home and I vowed I would never pray again. I hated the kind of God who took the credit when something good happened but when something bad occurred let it be said to be Man made.

This hatred for God continued for a few months and because it had set me thinking on a new line, I gradually realized I did not believe in God anymore. I thought 'how silly to hate someone who does not exist' and the anger went away and I became me again. I became the 'me' I was before having been taught about God. With no God and no school I felt free again to think my own thoughts. Throughout my entire life, reading has been taboo to me and in fifty-odd years and with great effort I have read only about six books. After a page or two of reading I become physically sick and I always thought it a terrible waste of time to read other people's thoughts when you could be thinking your own. So my mind was now empty and I alone could be responsible for deciding what ideas should be its new occupants.

It was at this stage of my life that I really noticed what was taking place. *I became aware of having knowledge of events before they happened.* There were many more children returning home from evacuation and we were in the habit of banding together and going about in groups, boys, girls, younger brothers and sisters. At this time of the war, there was a break in the bombing, which turned out to be the quiet before the storm as we still had the V1 doodlebugs to come. We children needed each other. When it was too dangerous to go far from home, we would all meet behind the air raid shelters. This was our favourite spot for chopping up fire wood to sell in bundles to earn extra pocket money. It was at several of those meetings that I would describe to the other children something that I could see and know was going to happen. These were things I could not possibly have known about and when they occurred I would lie in bed wondering and worrying how it was I could have possibly known. I would become very frightened. Fortunately, children in a crowd do not remember all that has been said and only I was aware of the sequence of events.

One example occurred when I spoke to a boy who I knew was stealing empty milk bottles from outside a little grocery shop to get the twopence back for each one. I told him that he would be caught by the owner, because he wouldn't see her. She came up behind him unexpectedly the next day and caught him in the act.

On other occasions I would often tell the children which

22

family would be the next to return home from evacuation. Invariably I was right.

It was the ambition of each and every one of us, boys and girls alike, to save up and buy roller skates. There was a very large flat open space nearby which many children used as a skating rink. We were all quite desperate to join in the fun and also to use roller skates on our many trips to the shops whilst going on errands. I found it almost impossible to save the amount required for skates, so I thought and visualized and really believed that someone would give me a pair. One particular day I continued this line of thought for well over an hour and just could not believe it when a better-off friend called and asked if I would like his old skates as he had bought new ones. After this event, if I needed something very much, I would follow the same procedure and *I got what I desired,* but always by very matter of fact, down-to-earth means.

I naturally wanted to share this way of getting things and one day I told two of my friends what to do if they really and truly wanted something. I explained that you couldn't just say, 'I want a jam tart' and one would appear. You had to want it so badly, with all your heart. The result of telling my friends was ridicule and remarks that I had gone funny in the head, so I made a joke of it and said, 'You really believed me. I really got you going.'

I had got out of my predicament but had sent myself into a deeper state of worry as to why I was so different from other children. When I told them, I had hoped they would say, 'Yes, we do that too,' but I understood this was not so and I really worried that I was funny in the head. No matter what I thought or they thought, this kind of thing still continued to happen. I asked myself, 'If you are actually in possession of the item you wished for, then how could it be connected with madness?' I never spoke about this to anyone again, although it continued, but I now wanted to spend more and more time on my own, thinking. As when I was very small, my favourite pastime was studying other children and even grown ups and just thinking about the things they did or said, trying to imagine if I would have done or said the same if I had been them instead of me. I so much hated being different from other children. I had no one in the world to talk to about my problem. My parents, brothers and sisters were too much

23

involved with the problems due to the war and even though we were all close, there was no one to whom I could speak about personal matters.

With each event my worries were growing and I would go to bed early so that I could think about the strange things taking place. Coincidence had to be ruled out, as by now I knew I could make things happen. At the age of twelve I was old enough to realize something very peculiar was happening to me and to no one else. Even the game I invented to play with my brothers and sisters made me feel different. I would go out of the room and they would agree on an object to concentrate on. Then I'd come back into the room and always knew immediately what it was they had chosen – it came straight into my mind. We played this the other way round too, for sometimes one of the others would go outside and I'd get the rest to concentrate with me on making them do some particular thing when they came back in, like picking up a certain object or saying something. It happened again and again and I knew I was causing it to happen.

As I have already said, we children went about in groups and some of the crowd were younger brothers and sisters whom our parents had made us take along. If an elder brother or sister was annoyed with always having a younger member of the family with them, then once away from home they would have a go at them and make them cry. The younger ones always came to me to protect them and then argued amongst themselves as to who would walk either side of me. It was not unusual for them to knock at my door and ask me to go out with them when they were not with older brothers or sisters. I would go, even though it made me the joke of the family. I could not turn them away. Whereas at the age of three to five I had been embarrassed to be seen with little children, I now felt totally different and realized that they needed me as if I were an adult. Although at that time people were not in the habit of inviting callers into their home as it was the practice to talk at the front door, I found that I made many friends among the parents of the small children I accompanied. I felt I had more in common with them than those of my own age.

After about a year or more of this kind of life, very slowly the schools began to re-open and along with several others I put

24

my name down to attend a nearby school. We were all fed up with the emptiness of having nothing of importance to do each day. I was able to bring my three Rs up to a reasonable standard and then, at fourteen, it was time to leave school behind and go into the world of work. Each of us knew this meant working in a factory, the same as our older brothers and sisters.

My first employment was in a munitions factory where I was trained on the drilling machines.

So ended my childhood days.

2

Now that I was out in the adult world I naturally had to make many adjustments to my life. For a while my mind was pre-occupied with practical matters and diverted away from the many hours I was used to spending in more abstract thought. Even before sleep I would be thinking about work the following day; so it appeared I was having a break from the unusual events of the sort described in Chapter One. However, there was certainly no break from the war, as the bombing had begun again with a vengeance. The munitions factory in which I worked was a natural target, so there were many interruptions during our working hours, back and forth to the air raid shelters provided for the workers. The strange thing is, that although I knew many people who were killed during the bombing I never felt sorry for any of the victims themselves – other than Billy Short for whose death I felt responsible – only for their families they left behind.

Taking into consideration that I was only a child at that time, I had an inner feeling, in spite of not believing in God, that they had all now gone somewhere pleasant. I had the strange idea that it was where we had come from before birth – and that someone or something was waiting for their return, which death on Earth brought about. This feeling had nothing whatsoever to do with the teachings I had received about God, heaven or hell. Sometimes I would have momentary flashes of remembering something, then nothing, but this thought has remained throughout my life. Now that I was working, I found that I gradually lost contact with school friends. Either they hadn't yet left school or they were, like me, working very long hours; with the air raids at night there was little time to meet. However, there were other fourteen-year-olds working and training with me in the factory. In fact we still used to take comics to work to read and swop: that's how immature we were. But, of course, the other youngsters lived in a large radius of the factory so we never made any arrangements to meet after working hours. Unlike the others, I seemed to get on very well with many of the older workers and during our breaks I gradually found I was preferring their company and listening to what they had to say rather than joking with those of my own age. For the first time I was hearing everyday accounts of the adult world and I was intrigued and began to think again and look into what had been said.

The bombing was followed by the doodlebug episode and then the V2 rockets. They caused immense devastation – but life goes on, and finally the war was over. I was now sixteen and a half. I settled into a normal job for munitions were now no longer needed and the factories were changing back to their pre-war production. During the next three and a half years I still preferred to be alone and returned again to the habit of thinking and going over in my mind all the events of my life. The more I thought about them the more different I felt. I would only have to hear a whisper about someone having been to a fortune teller or a medium for me to want to know all the details in the hope that I was gifted in the same way and not totally different from absolutely everyone else. I would still be disillusioned, however, because they always insinuated that they were in contact with people who had passed away, whereas my capability lay in influencing down-to-earth and day-to-day happenings. Although my 'events' were incredible they were not of the spiritualist type, and I always knew I was not as they were. I had no connection with the dead, only the living, and when I made a prediction I had no control over when I could do it – it came to me out of the blue and of its own accord.

I also found I became irritable if, when in conversation with people, they repeated or made a long story about anything as I had the picture long before they had finished and had 'seen' all my thoughts on the subject. It was as though I had heard their story and in a kind of a flash had viewed the situation in my mind. Seeing many angles at one and the same time. Some people, however, told a long story and had nothing to say, and I would know this before they had finished. I hated gossip and

27

probably revealed this fact as I constantly tried to change the subject. Talk about food also bored me. I have always preferred a sandwich to a full dinner. Even today I find what I eat of very little importance and rarely bother with cooked meals. When listening to other people discussing food I think that perhaps I haven't any taste buds; or perhaps food was so scarce in my early years that I subconsciously avoided taking more than I was entitled to. The odd thing is that during the periods that I ate very little food so many more of the strange events of my life occurred.

At this time it was all the rage for groups of people to get together and, using letters around a mirror and a small glass, to try to get messages 'from the other world'. I imagine that as so many people had lost loved ones during the war they were desperate for contact with them and for some sort of peace of mind. I attended several of these gatherings and although I must admit sometimes something would come through, startling those present. I always felt sure there was a very simple and logical answer to explain what had occurred. But at least it gave me something to think about, along with the conversations that took place after the meeting and how each person had reacted.

I still had glimpses into my future and on several occasions I knew what a person was going to say before they had said it, which I guessed was mind reading. It is strange but although I could will the things I wanted, I never asked for money as I never really had any desire for the things money could buy. I did, however, have a very strong feeling of not really belonging anywhere. I think I became quite sullen and unsociable at home although whenever an important change was to be made around the house it was always me that set about the task and accomplished it, never my older brothers or sisters.

One evening I was sitting in a theatre when, without an atom of doubt, I knew I was going to live in a foreign country, a desert area, in the not too distant future. But I could see no possible way for this to happen. A short time later I applied for a different kind of job which entailed sitting an exam. Having had very little formal education I felt sure I would not pass, but of the eight who took the exam I was one of the successful candidates. After months of training and courses I was unexpectedly sent to Africa as a business machine operator. So once again the future I had seen came true.

My deep thinking still continued and I tried to decide if I had really seen the future or had I desired to go abroad and made it happen? I had to reject the latter because the vision in my first awareness was of the exact place to which I went whereas I might have been sent to any one of a whole range of different locations which would not have tallied.

Once away from all those I knew and among complete strangers, I decided it would be a wonderful opportunity to change myself from what I had been in England. After an illness I lost a lot of weight and I changed my name, just my Christian name, so that I could actually feel I was a different person. This I managed to do for several months but then the old me came through, much to my dismay. Once again I tried to keep my thoughts to myself as much as was possible. The fact that I was now no longer so painfully shy meant I was always ready for a party, a joke or anything. But still the many little events continued; I had only to think of something and the very next minute someone would say it. Yet I had no reason to think in advance about what was said as it really meant nothing to me. These I called my 'compulsive thoughts', as they came to me without my wanting or needing them.

It was about this time that I felt very depressed about the whole affair and I wrote the following words. I recalled having written them earlier this year. These words represented a truth I could not deny and I knew it was impossible to run away as I thought I had done.

Escape
I tried to run away one day
So I hid behind a tree.
I wanted peace and solitude
I wanted to be free.

Then once again I tried to run
To escape my enemy
So I travelled miles across the land
I sailed the mighty sea.
My name I changed

My face grew thin
My friends I chose anew.
Then my foe looked in.

He had run with me
When I had run
He'd sat behind that tree
My Enemy is not a man
My Enemy is me.

I sincerely felt I had summed up my situation and although I was forever trying to learn of someone else who had similar experiences to mine, I knew I had to face the fact that I was different – and had to learn to live with it. As my 'difference' had on so many occasions worked to advantage, what was there to lose? But I always said to myself, 'Why me?' I often thought I would have been better off with a physical handicap as people could see and accept it – but how could anyone be expected to understand this? More importantly, who could I dare tell?

Over the years I found I had lost the desire to tell too much to anyone, always fearing ridicule. I hid all my true self by turning a situation into a joke or pretending to be insensitive to real-life concerns. Because of this, I was invited to many parties and gatherings as I was game for anything. Anything that made me stop feeling so different. Life at that time was a round of parties, always an excuse to celebrate something or other. I was courting steadily although not seriously enough to consider marriage, just a regular boyfriend. Because of this we went to many dances and even more parties among his friends, so for quite a few months all carried on quite smoothly and what with my work there was very little time to think about anything.

It was on the 25th November, my twenty-third birthday, when I flew home. My appointment overseas had come to an end and my replacement had arrived. I was once again working in a government office in London. I felt so restless that when an opportunity came up for another trip abroad I took it. Now I headed for the Far East.

I spent six weeks on the boat. Whenever we stopped off on the way or passed different countries all the other passengers became excited. They would go on deck or look forward to going ashore. If we weren't going ashore I would not even bother to go on deck, but would be contented to lie on my bunk in the cabin. However, if we were able to land for a few hours, in India for instance, I couldn't really make myself conspicuous to my fellow travellers by not going. I somehow felt nothing concerned me and even the fact of this indifference added to my worry about being apart from the rest.

It seemed – though this was not the case – as if I'd seen it all before. Why couldn't I get excited like everyone else? It was the chance of a lifetime . . . .

Because of all that was taking place in my life I never wanted to become close to any one person, always preferring to be part of a crowd of completely alone. I lost the desire to tell even important events, in case I slipped up and added something I would find hard to explain. Throughout even my adult life I have continued to do likewise.

It was during this second tour abroad that I was to become aware of events that concerned my family back in England prior to receiving the news by letters that arrived later, confirming my knowledge. On one occasion I knew something serious was wrong with my father, only for it to be confirmed a week or so later when a telegram arrived. Although I made every attempt to avoid giving away my knowledge of future events to my associates, this was not always possible. Sometimes I would jokingly make a statement only to find it to be a reality a short time later. This too has continued to occur throughout my life.

On one such occasion while living abroad, friends and I were killing time walking through a cemetery and I jokingly pointed to the only vacant plot in the area we were walking and said 'Look, that's being saved for me.' Just four hours later I was rushed to hospital by ambulance having caught dysentery through having drunk from a bottle that was contaminated with infected water. I had purchased the drink after leaving the cemetery. I was very ill and weighed only six stone and a few pounds when I came out of hospital four weeks later.

Because these kinds of events had taken place on too many occasions during my life there was just no way I could put them down to coincidence and had to include them in the many hours I would spend trying to sort out in my mind what was happening in my life that did not appear to happen to other people.

I could not help but conclude that it was all somehow connected with my thinking sessions and decided to eliminate them for a while. I did, however, continue to study and try to analyse the people I worked with, hoping as ever to meet or discover someone who had experienced something similar to me. This was not to be, so I kept up the 'couldn't-care-less-about-anything' attitude to life. Throughout my life I have loved any kind of challenge so I did not apply this attitude where my work was concerned. I may well have felt inferior because of my lack of formal education and therefore wanted to prove I was as capable as the next person.

I had also realized by now, if only subconsciously, that I was always made aware of an important part of my future which was yet to come after the making of a compulsive statement. This happened again the day a group of friends and I were discussing our future plans and what we intended to do when we returned to England. I was unexpectedly asked what my plans were. Without thought or hesitation I said, 'I am going to get married and have two babies before I am thirty years old.' So definite, so positive was the statement that I was terribly embarrassed and had to walk away from the group. Although dating was a constant on-and-off pastime for all of us, it was a known fact that I had no boyfriend in England, nor was I serious with those I was dating. I was twenty-four years of age. Was this again my destiny being revealed in advance?

I had at this time of my life realized that many of the strange incidents seemed to concern certain people who were connected in some way or other with my life at the time the events occurred. It was as though our minds had become joined in some strange way, and yet other people, with whom I was in contact as much as them, and sometimes even more so, played no part in my experiences. I came to the conclusion that maybe there were many different wavelengths that our minds dwell on and those that were to play a role in my life were on the same wavelength as myself. But then some even more bizarre event would occur, and this theory had to be discarded.

I actually began to dislike these certain people and would avoid their company as much as possible, and yet at the same time wanted to see what would happen next, so I would still find myself joining the company of which one or the other of these people were a part. To overcome this problem I made a point of avoiding being alone with them, but willingly joined in when several people were to be present. So mixed up was my thinking at this stage of my life, that in spite of my dislike of alcohol I attended as many parties as possible, so that because of the drink I had consumed I would fall asleep instead of thinking about my way of life. I somehow felt that these nightly thinking sessions were in some way connected with all that was taking place.

3

Once back in England I did not know what I wanted. Having travelled so much, life now seemed a bore; back to the old routine and England's uncertain weather. Although I had no wish to travel for a long time, if ever, I still felt restless. I was back working in a London office, but not the previous one. I cannot recall if anything particularly unusual happened except a flow of very minor events, the sort of things that happen to most people from time to time, known as 'coincidences'. This way of life continued for several months. I was dating, but not seriously.

That June, my boyfriend and I were invited to a house party which we attended along with two other couples. It was at this party I was to meet John, the man I knew I would marry if he were to ask me. This he did, just three months after our meeting and we married five months later. I gave birth to my second child in March 1958 and I was thirty years of age the following November. Another prediction had come true.

John and I had so much in common, we had both travelled to various places and were both compulsive workers willing to take chances rather than settle for the old run of the mill way of life that most people were content to go along with. At the early stage of my marriage to John, I had very cautiously discussed the strange events that had been taking place in my life, but soon realized it was not something he cared to discuss in great detail. Secretly I was pleased with his attitude and I hoped that now I was married and had young children to care for my strange way of life would all be in the past. Just after the birth of our first child we took out a mortgage and purchased a house which was in very bad condition. John, however, was a very capable man and learned new skills very quickly; he was able to make all the necessary alterations to the property to make our home one to be proud of. He had a very high-paid job and although it meant he had to spend periods of time working away from home, we did not mind, because the extra money enabled us to improve our property so much more quickly. Having completed all the work required and having been in one place for two years or more, John and I felt once again the desire to go abroad for a year or so, even though our babies were just one and two years of age. We decided to rent our house on yearly agreements and go to Canada for a couple of years. We both realized that we were not entirely free of the travelling bug and if we were to travel again, then it was better now than later when the children's schooling would be interrupted.

So, John went to Canada ahead of me to prepare for the children and me to arrive later. While John was in Canada looking for work and preparing a flat to accommodate us, I made arrangements with an estate agent for the renting of our house and the payments of mortgage from rents obtained. It was to be some four months after John had left England that the children and I were to follow.

During the discussion John and I had, prior to our deciding to go abroad, we both agreed how we felt obligated to the mortgage company and how we would endeavour to pay this debt as soon as was possible. This added to our reason to go to Canada in the hope of saving up and on our return to England being in a position to be able to rid ourselves of this debt. John at that time was a scaffolder and feared he might not get employment as such in Canada. This was his main concern. Then I made one of my compulsive statements. I said to John, 'It doesn't matter, because you are going to get the money we need repairing cars. It's just something I feel,' I added quickly.

Prior to John leaving for Canada our lives had been so full of the many tasks that were involved with bringing up two young babies, purchasing the house and all the alterations that were carried out on the property. Now, however, I was alone with my two young children and had all the time in the world to think about what the future in Canada would hold for us. We had spent all John's earnings on the house and the remainder was used for John's fare to Canada and a little for him to live on while settling in and finding employment. He

35

intended to borrow the fares for the children and me from the Canadian government.

I desperately wished I could raise the money we needed so that we would not have to start off our time in Canada in debt. We had decided that I would sell off some of the contents of our home to raise money for clothing that the children and I would require for the cold winter in Canada. I desperately tried to think of ways to make money and not have to do so.

Having two young babies and no one to talk to, I made it a practice to go to bed early. Sometimes I would purchase a magazine to glance through before going to sleep and often wished at this time that I could read books, as it would have passed the long evenings more constructively. It was in one of these magazines that I spotted an article in which three men, who wished not to be named, had written the story of how they would actually dream the winners of the following day's race meeting. It was explained in the article that you must never study the horses that are to run the following day, but take a pen and pad into the bedroom and make yourself wake up in the night to jot down your dream before you forget it. Next morning you must eliminate all parts of the dream that you are able to account for through having spoken of, or read about or heard mentioned prior to the dream having taken place. The part of your dream that you truthfully cannot account for, is your winner.

Prior to reading this article, I seldom dreamed at all, or if I did, I certainly did not recall doing so. But I did have to get up during the course of each night to feed the baby.

I felt desperate, excited and determined, and because of the kind of life I had led, with all its strange events, I believed that I too could dream the winners. And so began one of the most exciting and profitable periods of my life. I must point out that only on one occasion did I ever actually dream the exact name of the horse. The many winners I backed were, as the men had explained, concealed in dreams that concerned facts of my life at that time. I have in my possession a list of many of the winners I had during that period and these may easily be checked upon by looking up old newspapers and confirming that they did indeed win. However, I will give an example of one such dream to show how I selected the winner.

My dream

I dreamt I had actually arrived in Canada and I was in what appeared to be a hospital ward. There were beds down each side and I was unaware if the beds were occupied or empty. I was standing in front of a woman who was seated at a table in the centre of the ward. Although I did not hear her speak I was aware that she had accused me of having stolen something. I did not say a word and inside did not feel upset at her accusations because I knew I was innocent. At this point I awoke. The next day I purchased a paper and easily found my winner.

'NOT GUILTY' It won at 8-1.

The dreaming of winners continued for several weeks, averaging two per week. I was naturally very excited and wished other members of my family to make money as a result of my dreams, so on two occasions I informed them of the name of the horse which had resulted from yet other dreams. On both occasions the horse was taken out of the race prior to it being run, and I realized I was not meant to tell. During this period none of my dream winners lost or even came second. They all came first.

I also noticed that invariably the horse won at 2-1, 4-1, 8-1 and 16-1. Also that the winner was always in the 3 pm, 3.30 pm, 3.15 pm or the 3.45 pm race and never any other.

I raised all the money I required before leaving for Canada.

John was naturally very pleased when I joined him in Canada and presented him with all the winnings less what I had spent on clothing and other items that the children and I needed. *But,* if ever I dared to begin to tell anyone about my dream winners whilst in the company of John he would change the subject very quickly and never once in twenty-six years of marriage did he ever refer to the event. The whole subject was taboo.

After John had arrived in Canada he found it impossible to get employment as a scaffolder and seriously considered returning to England, as it was a very bad year in Canada and soup kitchens were opened to feed the many people who were unemployed. While John was out as usual searching for work, he spotted a garage that had the same name as an old friend of his back here in England. He approached the owner and asked was it possible he was related to his friend? He was indeed the same man's brother who had gone to Canada some ten years earlier. He employed John as a car mechanic.

We stayed in Canada for almost three years during which time, apart from working in the garage, John also took on private work repairing English cars. When we returned to England we had accumulated enough money to pay off our mortgage. *Just as I had predicted, the money had in fact come from cars.*

When one is living in a strange country for a certain period of time, it is very natural to think ahead to the year when you will be returning to your homeland. This I did most of the time while living in Canada, as the winters were far too cold for me to wish to stay one moment longer than was necessary. It is also very natural to try to visualize what will take place on your return and think about your family.

All this I did constantly. About two years prior to our intended return to England, John, our daughters and I were watching television. I was not particularly interested in the show and my thoughts once again had drifted off to when we were to go home. In spite of all the many events of my life, what took place then astounded me, and even though it was almost a forbidden subject as far as John was concerned, I blurted out all that I had suddenly become aware of. We had never once at that time considered selling the house we owned in England on our return, so there was no reason for my sudden knowledge. I said, 'John, when we get home we are going to buy this very big house. It has a large front door and hall and a large flight of stairs to the right of the front door that wind round to the upper rooms.' I picked up an empty white shoe box and said, 'I will try to draw you the hallway.' But, as I began to draw what I had seen, the hallway suddenly changed and now I could not see the stairway any more. I said to John, 'Something has been put in front of the stairs and I don't know what it is. It may be a settee or a column or something.' John's reaction was to continue to watch television, whilst I knew I had seen our future home. The house we owned in England had very little in the way of garden space and although I had not seen the garden of my vision house I knew it would be quite a size. Six months before we were due to return to England I insisted that John and I queue up at a large store for over an hour to purchase four very large reclining garden chairs that were on special offer, to take home to England for the house I knew we would own. I have photographs of these very same chairs in the garden of my vision house that we did buy and I still do live in. I will give further details of this a little later on.

One day, about nine months before we were to sail for England, I had been busy all day preparing for friends who were due to call that evening. As usual I was thinking of all that we would have to do to prepare for our return to England. Large packing cases had to be sent off long before we left so that they would be there upon our arrival. Once again I became fully aware of events that would take place on our return. So certain was the knowledge that it was as though I were thinking of past events rather than future ones. After having eaten a meal, John and I and our friends sat talking and because of something that was mentioned in the course of the conversation I suddenly recalled what had taken place earlier that day. I did not care if what I intended to relate would upset John, because I wanted proof of my predictions. I said, 'Soon after our return to England John and I will be separated for six months, and also John will be charged with having taken plants out of someone's garden.' John turned what I had predicted into a joke to cover up what I was saying, but I continued to say that, 'two baby girls will be born into my side of the family and I can only assume they will be twins.' Once again John, wanting to ridicule what I had said, went through each member of my family, and even I had to admit that because of circumstances and age it was not really likely to occur.

We returned to England in June of 1962.

Within a year of our return John was compelled because of circumstances beyond our control to live apart from the girls and me. Although I am able to prove these facts, it would not be fair to include details, but the party concerned did in fact counter charge John in a court of law for having removed plants from the garden. John won the court cases in both instances after six months of living apart.

While all this was happening, we were notified that two

39

sisters of mine were in fact pregnant and each gave birth to a daughter. One sister was unattached at the time of my prediction and the other was over forty years of age when she conceived. John refused to acknowledge the fact that my predictions had come true.

Now, although I appear critical of John's reactions this was not entirely so. I felt extremely disappointed, that having proved to John on several occasions that something strange was taking place, his unwillingness to discuss the matter made me realize that I would never find anyone to assist me in my search for the truth. At the same time I appreciated that John had no idea whatsoever that my whole life had been so involved in these kind of events, so why should he have concerned himself based purely on the little he knew? Why indeed should anyone?

It must be remembered that while many people played a role in my life, each one on an individual basis held only an atom of knowledge compared to all I was aware of. Having arrived at this conclusion I knew that only I and no one else could find the answers, as no one else had firsthand knowledge of the events, feelings and full results of all that was taking place in my life, any more than I am aware of any one elses full existence. There and then I knew that one day without help from anyone I would research and note all the details of all future events, and I would find the answers I was seeking.

4

During the course of the year following our return from Canada John had the security of a well paid job. We had re-modernized our house and had decided to save as much money as possible for two years or so, and then sell our house and purchase a better one.

In November of 1963 I was to meet a person who would become involved in many more and new kinds of 'events' that were to occur in my life. Kay and I met in our nearby shopping centre. We were both choosing Christmas tree decoration, and once served, we left the store together. It turned out that Kay lived very near to my home, so we walked home together. Although Kay was quite a bit older than myself we quickly became friends, as did John and Kay's husband Ted. It was after an evening the four of us had spent together that John informed me that Ted and Kay had lost their only child, a son, when he was killed on a motor bike. John was not sure of the exact details but it sounded as though the boy was racing at the time of his death. Although Kay and I spent many afternoons together, I never once mentioned or enquired about her son, knowing that if she wished to tell me she would do so in her own time.

During the early stage of our friendship I became aware that Kay was yet another person such as those I spoke of earlier, that had in some way become connected with my mind, on the same 'wavelength'. At many of our meetings Kay would discuss the very thing I had been either doing, or thinking of doing, prior to the meeting having taken place; and I too would answer her queries before she had cause to mention them. One day I had searched every store to purchase a certain kind of slip I required, but having no success in doing so, I decided to call on Kay on my way home. Kay was very

41

pleased to see me because, as she explained, 'I bought this slip several months ago and shall never wear it. Would you like it?' It was the very same kind of slip I had been searching the shops for. That night, before going to sleep, I thought over all the events that had been occurring since our friendship began, and that night I was to dream my first 'special' dream. These dreams were vivid, clear and meaningful ones, so much so that I knew they were special. (Those I had when dreaming the winners were completely different.)

In my dream I was travelling along a sunny country lane in what must have been a car, but there was no window blocking my view of the countryside. I was in the passenger seat and was not aware who was driving the car. Across the field I could see a white sheet on the grass and told the driver what I could see. Then I was walking towards the sheet. I lifted it up and underneath was a young boy in his early teens. He had a lovely suntan and very rosy cheeks. His hair was black and I could see the comb marks in the Brylcream or whatever dressing he had on it. He looked as though he were asleep, but I knew he was dead. I stood upright and looked across the field in which I was standing and saw about six policemen riding towards me on bicycles. I did not see them pass me but, still looking across the field, I could now see a church and a coloured vicar standing in the doorway. On the roof of the church a fat lady was edging her way down the slates. Her dress was pulling up as she moved and showing her stocking tops. I assumed that the church was on fire and she was trying to escape.

The day following this dream it was my turn to call on Kay. While chatting I decided to tell her about the strange dream. Kay's face remained expressionless as I spoke, but when I had told her the whole dream she said very softly, 'You saw the death of my son.' Now for the first time, she wanted to speak about him. She told me how her son, Glen, and his friend, and Ted and herself had all been away on a lovely holiday, the boys on their motor bikes and she and Ted in their open sports car. On the way home they were driving slowly through the countryside chatting to the boys who were riding beside them. All were agreeing it had been a lovely holiday. Glen's friend then went on ahead of them down the lane and disappeared round a bend. Glen followed his friend, but as he reached the bend his motor bike hit a bump in the road and threw him into a field. He died instantly. Kay went on to say that all she remembers after that was being surrounded by policemen and getting into an ambulance.

After Glen's death she and Ted joined a spiritualist church and regularly went to a medium and received messages from Glen. The vicar of the church was a coloured man, and the medium was just as I described the lady on the roof.

Kay was so sure that I was a medium and a very good one, that she tried to persuade me to go to the meeting with them. I tried to explain I was different from mediums because 'they contact the dead, and I contact the living.' There was no way I could tell her I did not believe in the so-called powers of mediums and destroy something she believed in. However, that evening for the first time ever I had to admit to myself that it was a possibility that I was a medium, and was just stubbornly refusing to believe it. Maybe the other people who were connected to my thoughts were of the spiritualist faith also, and this was the reason our minds joined in some kind of bond. Because of these new thoughts, when Kay and Ted arranged to attend a meeting being held by a well-known medium, I agreed to go with them. The few people in the audience to whom the medium gave messages were certainly able to verify his knowledge of their departed relatives, and even though the messages from their loved ones were rather pathetic and unimpressive, they were delighted.

But in no way, no way was I connected with what I had witnessed that evening. How easy it would have been for me to accept all this as the truth I was seeking. If the medium had been a complete failure, it would not have made my search for the truth so very complicated. But because he certainly did have something to offer his followers, I had to include in my research that somehow and in some way spiritualism did in fact have some kind of connection.

Over a period of time, human beings have the ability to eventually accept almost anything that they cannot alter. We 'learn to live with it'. This is how I managed to cope with my difference, by accepting it, but I could never give up the constant search in my mind to find out why and how. With each new 'event' I spent more and more time going over all the circumstances and the associated feelings. I tried to seek out books on the subject of the mind, but as soon as I had read two or three pages I would be overwhelmed with nausea, as though I had a sort of jet-lag. This had been the case throughout my life. I realized if I were to own a hundred books that they would be of little use. Anyway, I had an awareness that was not easy to think about – that I already had all the answers inside me and that no book or person could ever show me this truth. My purpose in life was to find it myself. Everything I had ever sincerely desired had materialized so why not this also?

By May 1965, my daughters were seven and eight years of age and we had been home from Canada more than two years. It was usual, if I needed something from our local shops for me to ask the girls to go on their return from school. I was extremely busy one day and remembered I did need a little shopping done. I thought of asking the girls to go when they arrived home but I had a very strong feeling that on this occasion I must not send the girls, but go myself. For fear that I would have cause to regret sending them, and in spite of the fact that my new shoes hurt, I hobbled to the shops. The shop assistant was standing in the entrance talking to a customer and while waiting to get by and enter the shop I could not help but overhear their discussion. The customer was saying, 'I don't know what we shall do, we are only a few weeks from moving into our new house and now we have heard the buyer of our house cannot get a mortgage.' The assistant walked into the shop and the customer towards the kerb to cross the main road. On impulse I walked over to the customer and said, 'Excuse me, do you have a house to sell, as my husband and I may be interested?'

She said, 'Yes, it is that large corner house across the road,' and pointed to a very large and obviously run-down piece of property. Taking up her offer to view the house we crossed the road and entered the house. I stood dumb-struck. I was standing in the hall of my vision house. The one I had been made aware of several years previously in Canada.

I said to the woman, 'I am not going to view the house until I can contact my husband to view it with me. I shall be back very soon.' I could hardly contain myself as I crossed back over the road to the telephone box to phone my husband's place of work. Now if you were to have known my husband you would soon have learnt that he was not the kind of man to drop what he was doing and leave his work without a very good reason for doing so. On this occasion, however, all I said to him was, 'Would you come home? I have something to show you.'

He said, 'I will be with you in ten minutes.'

Together we returned to the house. It was as I had gathered, in a very bad condition but I knew we would own this property. John hardly said a word as we walked from room to room, then having looked all over this large house and its ten big rooms we were taken into the garden. This was large by our standards and at the far end of the garden stood a big brick garage. We were standing in the garage when John (without our usual discussion when we were about to embark on something of this nature) turned to the woman and said, 'If the price is right we will buy it.'

In June 1965 we moved into my vision house.

During the following two years my husband converted the house into two flats. He did this by cutting off the four bottom stairs that led to the upper rooms, turned them alongside the existing stairs and making two small landings to enable a continuation up the stairs to the upper flat, after first having cut a second front door. He then blanked off the stairs to separate the flats from each other by erecting a wall with a cupboard beneath. Now from our lower flat the stairs could not be seen. This was why I had said in Canada, 'Now I cannot see the stairway.' Because there was so much money to be spent on our new home, and in spite of having sold our first home, we were back in debt with a mortgage. John dearly wished to start up on his own in some kind of business. He decided to use the large garage in the back garden and set himself up in car repairs. This he did, but was not at all happy in the work. He needed to be away from the house, not always either working inside or on cars outside.

One evening he was particularly depressed about the whole situation and we sat discussing how to alter it. I said to him, 'What exactly would you like to do?'

He answered very positively, 'I would like to start on my own in factory maintenance.' I thought this over and decided, yes, this would be it. A short time after the conversation I had to go out for a while. I was still thinking of our discussion. When I returned home an hour or two later, John said to me,

'You are not going to believe what happened after you went out.' I thought, with my way of life, I believe anything. He then said how he went out to the front garden for some reason or other and outside our front door was a man trying to start up his car without any success. John offered to assist and started the car for him. They then stood talking. The man said to John, 'You don't by any chance know anything about maintenance work do you, as I am a foreman for a company that carries out factory maintenance work, and we are in a lot of bother with one of our contracts?' John was now out of the motor trade and well established working for himself on factory maintenance. John, being a very adaptable and capable man, progressed so much that between us we formed a limited company that proved a great success, and which we sold in 1973. This was by no means a big company, but was in every way suitable in size and beneficial to our particular lifestyle.

Throughout our marriage I assisted John in every way possible. We were a good team and whatever one could not do, the other one could. We were both hard workers, willing to take chances when the stakes were against us, and neither of us was really interested in show of any kind, whether it be clothes, expensive cars or anything that most people dream of being able to afford. We were content with the security we had accomplished, our home, children and our work. We could not exist without some challenge or other, so as each challenge was overcome we set ourselves new ones. I guess my challenge right now is the writing of this book, and because of my lack of word association it is proving to be the hardest challenge of my life. Because of all I have to reveal and in spite of the sickness and nausea I feel each time I begin a new page, I shall continue to write my story no matter what.

In spite of the fact that many small firms like ours were going out of business through lack of funds or unreliable labour, we continued to prosper. During the years that followed, very much was to take place in our lives concerning my strange events. Sometimes I felt that John and I had become united mentally and this was the reason that I was now to experience so many new abilities that were mainly in John's interest rather than mine. Whenever John needed something desperately I too would think profoundly and

46

determinedly about the item, rather than see John get so agitated. Over the years of desiring items by my individual method I came to realize that very few of the desires were actually mine; always John's. All that I have to relate now consists of many of my strange 'events' that on the surface appear to be separate individual happenings. This, however, is not so.

(Although it is not at all possible for me to express and give a clear understanding at the present time, I can assure you, the reader, that most of the events that I include in these writings do in fact connect together, repeat one another, and from within my mind present themselves in circles of circumstances.) Even the most minute incidents that connect to the main event are repetitions of those connected with other strange occurrences. Certain surnames, for instance, crop up on many occasions. Dates also play a very important part in my life. Number 9 is connected in some way or other to every important part of my life. In an earlier chapter I spoke of the second house I moved into after having left the East End of London. It was while living in that house that I became fully aware of the strangeness of my life. I moved into that house on my ninth birthday. The house number was 81; $8 + 1 = 9$; $9 \times 9 = 81$. In my private book of recollection I have listed much more detail on this subject; also the many times certain dates of the year have played a vital role in my strange life, but since I have no knowledge of astrology in any way, I find it pointless to include such details in this book. I just know from within that they are of great importance.

It was during the early months of having formed our company that John said to me one evening, 'Do you remember the electrical book I took out on loan from the library a while ago?' I said that I did and he went on to say it was absolutely vital that I went to the library to get it for him the following day as he needed it to help him with a complicated electrical contract that he had to complete before the weekend. Sensing his urgency I assured him I would definitely get him the book the following day.

At midday on the following day I was ready to go to the library to get the book he needed so desperately. I had rushed around all morning to carry out this task, and yet when I was about to leave the house I turned back and simply sat still on the settee with my coat on, for a whole hour. At 1 pm I made my way to the library. Because I am not familiar with such places and did not wish to disturb the librarians who appeared to be busy, I noted there was just one member of the public other than myself, a middle-aged man glancing through a book he had taken from the shelf, and I went over to him and asked if he could assist in helping me locate the book I required. I named the book and also added who it was written by, as John had written this information on a slip of paper the evening before. The man looked vaguely puzzled and said, 'It is not here. I have just happened to look for the same book.' This I just could not believe. Just two of us in the library, and out of millions of books, we both were interested in the same one. He saw the disbelief on my face and having placed the book he had been reading back on the shelf he turned to me and said, 'You don't believe me, come out of here with me and I shall prove it to you.'

We left the library together and I followed him to his car. He opened the door and from under the dashboard took a brown paper bag, from the bag he produced the very book I required. The man then said, 'I don't understand all this. I bought this book eight years ago and never once used it. It has remained on my book shelf ever since. Last night, however, I took the book from the shelf, put it in this bag and placed it in my car and I have no reason why I should have done this.' He then added, 'Another strange thing is that I have never before been in this library at this time of the day. Out of curiosity I looked on the shelf for the book before you arrived.' He asked if I wished to buy the book from him. I readily agreed. He asked if ten shillings was all right with me and I assured him it was. He then decided that he would write his name and address inside and should my husband not wish me to buy it he would return my money. His name was Mr Evans. I still have this book.

During the following two years Kay and I continued to meet regularly and although Kay held spiritualist meetings each Tuesday evening in her home I never wished to attend them. I did, however, call on Kay one day and found that she had company. Kay explained that she and Ted had offered to take this couple in their car with them a little later to the spiritualist meeting they were going to attend, and these were the mediums, a husband and wife who were to take the stage. Kay then told them that I too had special powers, and they asked if I was also a medium. I assured them I was not but did admit I had certain kinds of ability to relate what I should not know about other people. Not wanting to miss out on this golden opportunity I gave them a sitting, so to speak. They were astounded at all I was able to reveal about even their inner emotions and other personal details. The woman insisted that I was indeed a medium and a far better one than she or her husband, and pleaded with me to take the stage that evening instead of themselves. Of course I declined to do so since I am no hypocrite and would never admit even to myself that I was connected in any way with their beliefs.

Many times during the year that followed Kay would come to me after one of her spiritualist sessions and say how Glen had spoken to her and asked to give me messages from him. I would say how nice of him, or if she said he had sent her to me to assist her in any way I would go along with it.

The year following, John decided that it would be a good idea if we were to purchase a second house as an investment. From then on we decided to watch out for an appropriate one. One evening we had finished our meal and while John read the paper I washed up the dishes. I suddenly became quite alarmed because I was aware of the conversation that Kay and Ted were having in their home. I turned to John and said, 'I don't care if you believe me or not but I know at this moment Kay and Ted are discussing selling their house.'

'Never,' said John. 'Ted has constantly told me it would have to be over his dead body that their house was ever sold.'

'I don't care what you say.' I replied. 'The thing is, if they are selling are we interested in buying it?' As usual, if John was to be affected by my abilities, he was always interested.

'Why don't you visit Kay tomorrow and see if it is true?' he said.

The next day at 11 am I went to call on Kay. I said, 'Kay, I have told you about my strange abilities on many occasions and I want you to answer truthfully. Were you and Ted discussing selling this house last night?' She looked at me absolutely stunned and put her hand to her mouth. 'Ted will swear that I told you as only he and I know.' At 12 noon Ted came in to lunch. Kay looked at him sheepishly and told him that I knew they intended to sell the house. I said, 'Please believe me Ted, Kay did not tell me. I have spoken often enough about my abilities and this is how I came to know. To prove this, I can tell you right now that you and I are going to come into contact with two gold-coloured ashtrays.'

'But I don't have any gold ashtrays,' he replied.

'Neither do I,' I said. 'But we will.'

At a later meeting Ted confided in John that they were in financial difficulties and had no choice but to sell their house and purchase a cheaper one. During the course of that meeting John made an offer for the house which Ted said was very fair and accepted. We promised to assist them in looking for a house for them to purchase.

On the following Saturday John, the children and I were on our way to the shops in the car. While held up in the traffic I felt very uneasy because I had insisted that John stopped his work to go to the shops with me as I wished him to meet someone. I thought how angry he will be if the man is not in the shop when we get there. John interrupted my thoughts and said, 'Look!' I looked, and saw a house where a man was in the process of pinning a handmade FOR SALE notice in his window. John said, 'I bet Kay and Ted will be interested, let's stop on the way back and view the house for them.' Because of wishing to view the house, John was not annoyed that the man I had wanted him to meet was not there, and turned the car round and headed back to the house. A middle-aged man opened the door in response to our ringing the bell. John explained how we wished to view the house on behalf of our friends and be in a position to give them full details before they viewed it. The man invited us in and asked if we would mind waiting in the living room while he finished his telephone conversation in the next room. He went on to apologize for the room being empty, as all his belongings had already been moved to his new accommodation. There were just two items left on the mantelshelf in the room we entered: TWO GOLD ASHTRAYS. John was rather impressed with this house and said if it were reasonable enough we might be able to afford this one also if Kay and Ted were not interested. John and I were shown around by the owner and before we left John said to the man. 'If you are unable to sell at the price you are asking, I will make an offer right now that I am prepared to buy at. All you have to do is contact me.' The man said this was fine and produced a pen and pad to write down our name and phone number.

He was about to write the name down when he stopped, looked at me, and said, 'You have been in this house before.'

'No,' I replied. 'I never forget where I have been.'

'Of course not,' he said. 'I met you two years ago at the library and sold you an electrical book.' Mr Evans, of course.

Kay and Ted did not buy the house neither did we ever hear from the man.

About two weeks later when I had been on my weekly visit to Kay, I got up out of the chair to leave and for no apparent reason or thought, I looked at Kay and said, 'Has Ted made out his will?'

'No,' she said, looking puzzled, and then added, 'I would be in bother if anything was to happen to Ted.' I said goodbye and went home feeling rather annoyed with myself for having said such a thing. Just two evenings later John and I were watching the 10 pm news on television when our door bell rang. Two men who were strangers to us had come with the sad news that Ted had died of a heart attack earlier that day. We withdrew our offer in the hope that Kay could get a better price for her house, but it was finally sold for the same sum that we had offered. Just as Ted had said, it was sold 'over his dead body'.

After the death of Ted, Kay moved away to the coast and we never heard from her again. The book that I bought from Mr Evans I kept among my belongings rather than alongside John's other manuals on the book shelf.

About three years later I joined a social club and made many friends there. I would go about one evening a week at that time. I rarely discussed more than I felt was necessary about my strange happenings to the friends I had made, although there were occasions when one or other of them realized that something I had said did in fact occur a little later, or I would answer a question before having been asked it. From time to time someone would bring up the subject of fortune tellers or spiritualist meetings that were to take place

51

in a local hall. On one of these occasions a woman sitting nearby joined our conversation and I found that what she had to say on the subject interested me. I told her that I would like to meet her sometime and discuss her views. She agreed to call on me at my home one afternoon the following week. During this meeting we discussed various forms of unaccountable events that take place in people's lives and I confided in her many of those I had in fact experienced. I also explained to her how an inner feeling constantly insists that I am not, as so many people have insisted in the past, a medium. Then, for some unknown reason, I decided to tell her about the book and how I had come by it, and of my second meeting with Mr Evans. I took the book from the drawer having told her the story and passed it to her. Jane opened it and read Mr Evans's initials and name, and said, 'How strange, I lost my husband just a couple of years ago and he was also Mr H.G. Evans.'

The week after this incident I met a friend with whom I had also at an earlier date discussed a few of the events taking place in my life, and her first words on meeting were to tell me about a book she had recently read, and how she thought that I too would find it very interesting. It was *The Third Eye* written by Lobsam Rampa. Although it was alien to me to take a book from the library with the intention of reading it, I did so on this occasion, but once I had the book, the same old nausea came over me and I realized that to read it was out of the question. About ten days later I remembered I still had the book and returned it to the library unread. That evening I went to my social club for the first time since our meeting at my home, I met Jane. She called me over and said, 'Now I have a list of five books that you must read.'

I said, 'Jane, does one of them happen to be *The Third Eye?*'

She said, 'Yes, but how on earth could you have known that?' I then explained how useless it would be for me to take the list of books from her and how if I obtained them, I would be unable to read them.

Many years were to pass before I was to mention or show anyone this book again. In fact it was 1984 during the months prior to my findings being revealed to me.

As many as four people had said to me on various occasions that they disliked one particular room in my home because they felt strange sensations in there. I dismissed the allegations as ridiculous, but when one of them suggested that I get a medium to have a sitting in this room, I did agree, just to see how such people set about proving their so-called ability to contact 'the other side'. I left the finding of the medium to my friend Joan who had suggested the idea. After many phone calls, several weeks later she finally found a medium who was prepared to call at my house one evening the following week. I had invited a few other friends to make up a small gathering. On the very day that Mr and Mrs Sturd were to come for the sitting, Joan was taken ill and had to take to her bed. The whole evening was disastrous and they were unable to make any impression whatsoever. Mr and Mrs Sturd wished to carry out the sitting with just my presence, so my friends were left for over two hours sitting in another room. I knew how annoyed they would be and the guilt I felt about them not being included in the sitting made it impossible for me to take in what was being said. I had set a tape recorder up to make a recording of the sitting, but the following day I found the tape was blank and nothing had been recorded.

After my friends had finally gone home Mr and Mrs Sturd and I sat and discussed their beliefs and their powers to contact those now departed. I spoke of my abilities and after a long conversation on the subject they said how they envied me and how I had been given a wonderful gift that I should share with other people. Having had so much first-hand knowledge of the unusual in my own life, I understood that these people were not fakes in what they could do that convinced the general public. They were special kind of people, but being showmen and to enthrall their audience, they added a certain amount that was just not so. The better the showmen the more famous they became.

The next evening at the club, I met Joan, who wanted to know what had taken place, and said how disappointed she had been that she was unable to attend. A woman nearby heard the conversation and said how interested she too was in spiritualism. Being unable to talk in the club, she, like Jane arranged to call on me one afternoon. This she did, and we discussed various aspects of spiritualism. I made it quite clear that I did not believe in spiritualism, yet I too could describe a person now dead, and speak of events that had not yet taken place on certain occasions. For the second time under similar circumstances I had an impulse to speak of the book. Which I did, and then produced it for Debbie to inspect. She too read the name inside and said, 'My maiden name was Evans.' My friend Joan (Wallis) daughter's married name was also Evans. I suppose I felt very keen to prove myself to Debbie, and decided to attempt to tell her details about her life that were unknown to me. These were all correct. She then asked if I could speak of her future. Without hesitation I informed her that she was going to read, maybe in a letter, some very important news that would cause quite a shock to her.

I did not see Debbie again until 25th November, which was my birthday. As I walked into the club that evening she called me over and appeared excited. She then showed me a newspaper in which a woman was trying to trace her missing sister. Debbie was in fact the person she was seeking. Debbie now realized her parents were not her true parents and that she had many relatives by the name of Wallis. Debbie was then approached by a man who wished to take up the story of her new-found family. His name was Mr Sturd. A week or so later I had been told about a fortune teller who lived quite close to my home. She had a reputation for being very good and many people went to see her. I mentioned her to Joan (Wallis) and Debbie, and all three of us decided to pay her a visit. I came away so disgusted with what this woman had the audacity to offer for the money she took from her clients, that I knew I would never again donate a penny to such people, even out of curiosity. The only thing that I found interesting about the whole affair was the fact that the fortune teller's name was Debbie Wallis.

Just two months ago I had reason to take the deeds of my vision house, where I still live, from their safe keeping at the bank. Reading back to the very first occupier of this house I discovered it was none other than a Mrs Sturd. Her lease was signed on 29th December, 1909. So somehow, some way throughout the years, in just this one chain of many chains that were going on in my life the names Evans, Wallis and Sturd were all to be connected with a book.

Although those connected with these events are unaware of the writing of this book, once my findings are made known these people will surely verify my claims, and I can produce the book, the introduction card given to me by Mr and Mrs Sturd the mediums, and naturally the deeds to my house. Take just this one story and understand how each person who was to be involved with the events concerning this book holds one or two pieces of the puzzle, while I have been able to gather them all together to further the private research which has dominated my life.

So where exactly did this chain of circumstances really begin? During the years, I had included the events of this book into my mental search for the answers and had assumed the event began the day John so desperately required the book. At a later date I assumed that the visit to the fortune teller and her name connection was the end of the whole affair. Now I so recently discovered that it all began as long ago as the first occupier of my vision house. And was that not all another chain of events leading to the purchase of this house? So very many separate chains of events were taking place in my life, and all at one and the same time. Because it would be impossible for me to relate each and every one of my happenings, or to place them in the order in which they occurred, I shall select and devote a chapter or two to some of the many events that took place prior to 1984, that were to lead to the truth I had spent my life seeking.

5

As when I was a child, I still retained the ability to obtain by thought items that I desperately required, whether it be for myself or another member of my family. In this chapter I will relate some of these incidents.

Our firm continued to be successful although many small outfits around us went into liquidation one by one. We did, however, go through a very worrying period when the contracts we were working on were nearing completion with nothing to follow. John said he had been very concerned about this as he did not wish to lay off our good labour force. He went on to say, 'If only Mr Shaw would contact us again, that would be the answer.' Mr Shaw's work had made our company possible in the beginning but somehow over the years we had completely lost touch with him. I assured John that Mr Shaw would contact us to which he replied, 'I suppose you're going to work the Oracle again.' I laughed and pointed out that it was 11 pm and I was going to bed. The next morning I was thinking about John's remark and felt rather angry. Then the phone rang.

'Mr Shaw would like some work carried out? Yes, I will tell John to arrange a meeting.' I glanced at the clock and noted it was 11 am. Our problems were over and so was any mention of the fact that yet another of my statements had materialized within twelve hours.

One Saturday John and I spent all day on office work to get out a load of letters to surveyors, clients and suppliers, as well as preparing invoices for posting before the start of a new week. Having completed all the letters, I discovered that I had completely run out of the long white envelopes I required to send them away in. This meant that we could not post them that evening after all. John was rather annoyed that I had neglected to ensure we had a stock of stationery, and I thought 'I must find some, I must find some,' but I knew full well there were none around. At that moment the door bell rang and a neighbour whom we had little cause to associate with stood on the door step. She said to me, 'I have been clearing out a cupboard and wonder if these are of any use to you.' She passed me a handful of long white envelopes. (If asked, this neighbour would, I am sure verify this.)

On another occasion, just five days before Christmas, John was desperate to find an experienced decorator to finalize a contract that had to be completed before the Christmas recess. Neither of us knew such a person, and because I was about to go to my mother's home, a short bus ride away, I left the house wondering how we would solve the problem. For the short distance I had to travel I never made it a practice to go on the upper deck of the bus. This day, however, I did, and once seated took my cigarettes out and discovered my lighter had run out of fuel. A very elderly man sitting next to me kindly gave me a light. He then started chatting to me. He told me he was a retired painter and decorator and when I asked if he would be interested in some work he jumped at the opportunity. He completed the contract for us and stayed in our employment for several years.

Another time, my husband wanted a second-hand jumper to work in. He said a new one would be soiled within an hour, so would I ask around my family and if I have the choice of several look for a blue one with a slash neck. None of my family had such a jumper, but a couple of days later John came home from work and said he had found the jumper he required. It was his size, blue with a slash neck, second-hand, and he had found it in a bag that was lying in the middle of the road having obviously fallen from the back of a cleaner's vehicle.

My mother told me one day that she had ordered a new single bed from her local store, and she would be paying £10 for it. She said she wished to get rid of her double bed, replace it with the single one and later she would buy a small locker for the bedroom. I asked her why she had not discussed it with me first, and I pointed out that a bed for only £10 would be cheap and nasty. When I returned home from this visit to my mother I had been back a very short time when my door bell rang. I was very surprised to see that my visitor was a young man I had met only once before when he was with a friend of ours who came round some months before. He said he was passing and on impulse had decided to call. I made tea and he told me how he was in the process of moving out of his bedsit and into the home of an elderly couple as part of the family. He said he had sold his furniture but still had to sell an almost new single divan bed (which he had recently paid £30 for) and a bedside locker. He added that he would accept £10 for the two items. I bought them from him and after he had left telephoned the store my mother had ordered her bed from to cancel the order. This took place about 1970.

Because John and I drew limited salaries from the company so that we could build up our capital for investments, there were several times I desperately required an item for our home that we could not afford. On one of these occasions I desperately wanted floor length curtains to replace the very short and thin ones that hung in my two large bay windows. One day I decided I would get the necessary money somehow and felt so determined that I went to a large store, chose the appropriate curtain material, noted the price, returned home and measured my windows to find out how many yards of material would be required. Having done this I worked out exactly how much money I would need to buy the material. Then, before sleep each night, I determined I wanted and would acquire the sum of money required. It worked. I won the amount at my club just a week or so later. Then I decided I would like the same material for the back windows of my home and successfully followed the same procedure. Now, having purchased this vast amount of material who could I possibly find to make them up for me? With the material piled high on the table I sat contemplating my predicament when my door bell rang. Once again it was Terry, the young man who had sold me the bed and locker, and whom I had not seen in quite a while. I invited him in and when he saw the material he asked what it was for. I explained how I was not capable of making the curtains myself, to which he replied, 'That's no problem at all, mum, the lady I have moved in with does sewing to earn a little money.' Within an hour, complete with the required measurements, Terry had taken the material off in his car and once again my problem was solved. A week later Terry returned with the curtains all beautifully made up. I have never to this day seen Terry again.

Philip, the friend who had introduced us to Terry, lived further along the road from our home. Just two weeks after he had purchased a new car, John and I also purchased the same model in a different colour. I stood in the front garden about five months later and Philip waved to me as he passed by in his car. I went inside the house and said to John, 'Philip has just waved to me and all the side of his new car is smashed in.' John was shocked and wondered how it had happened. The very next day John met Philip and asked how he had damaged his car. Philip agreed he had waved to me, but said there was nothing wrong with his car, which he proved by showing it to John. A month later a police car chasing a stolen car came out of a side turning and smashed into the side of Philip's car.

One Christmas I had bought several gifts for each of my two daughters and had wrapped them. I did not know what else to get them, so decided to carefully unwrap the jewellery boxes and place £40 inside each of them. That evening I went to my club and won £80.

When my mother died, two sisters and I went to the undertaker's to make the funeral arrangements. I wrote out a cheque for £219. Two weeks later I won £219.

Six months later an uncle died and again I wrote out a cheque, but this time for £225. Two weeks later I had six wins that totalled £225.

Many times throughout the years this kind of event would occur and no one could possibly say it was merely coincidental.

In the midst of all that was going on in my life I spent many hours going over each occurrence. I took into consideration all the daily and natural events that were going on at the same time as all these strange happenings. Why, I asked myself so many times, could I never hear or meet anyone else that even remotely had similar occurrences? As always I still preferred to spend many hours alone, but the strange thing was that I never really felt alone. As my daughters grew older I soon realized that like John, they did not wish to discuss these events so in spite of occasions when I blurted out something of this nature, on the whole very little of what was taking place was discussed with them. I actually felt that it caused them embarrassment. Therefore, as in the past, there was absolutely no one to assist me in searching for the answers I was seeking.

I had no control whatsoever over most of the events that occurred, only those where I willed the result. Whenever something happened, such as a view of the future, it happened when I least expected it and invariably at a time when my mind was occupied with a problem or I was excited or angry about something. The idea of controlling events in any way was completely out of the question. Yet when a member of my family said they wanted something, even a very unusual item, I would confidently say, 'Leave it to me, I'll get it for you.' Some time later, usually within twenty-four hours, I'd be approached by someone with the exact item. I did not even have to look or make enquiries – just like the envelopes and the bed and locker incidents and so many, many more I could relate.

You would have thought people would be grateful for getting what they wanted, but unfortunately humans do not react this way. Just like John, they began to resent the fact I was able to achieve what they had failed to do. I experienced this kind of resentment many times, so over the years I became less and less involved with others and avoided family gatherings. This, however, took a lot of the spirit out of my life, as the one thing I got most pleasure from, was helping other people.

The most striking aspect about all I did was the utterly down-to-earth, matter-of-fact way it was so easily accomplished. This prompted such remarks from people as, 'You have the Midas touch', 'The luck of the devil' or 'If your face fits you can get anything'. And from a more thinking type of person, 'You are psychic', You have a spirit guide'. Each of the very few people in whom I confided more than I usually did, openly admitted how afraid they would be if such things happened to themselves, and asked how I could cope with the way things were. A long time ago I realized that although I had no power to change my way of life, I did have the power to change my attitude towards these events. So rather than fear them I considered each one as another piece of the puzzle I was trying to solve.

Whilst I can describe the events I find it impossible to

60

convey my inner feelings. When dreaming the winners for instance, I had a sure certainty, a kind of knowledge once I had the dream that the particular horse could only be a winner, so much so that I felt a cheat taking my winnings.

As I explained earlier, when I became aware of future events which I knew would take place, it was as though they had already occurred and I was merely in the process of recalling them. During the course of a discussion with several people who were investigating such phenomena, I happened to say: 'You know how you can feel which side of your brain you are thinking with? Well, I use the right side of my brain to get the things I require.' They told me they did not know which side of the brain they were using. I had thought everybody knew, and for the first time realized this was one of the differences between myself and other people.

Apart from being a compulsive thinker I am also a compulsive worker, and prefer work that entails a kind of relaxation enabling me to pursue my own thoughts at the same time. I am, and always have been in contact with many people, and although I may have given the impression of living the life of a hermit, this is very far from the truth. It is the *inner* me that remains private. My outward attitude to life is utterly different from my inner self. So much so that there hardly seems to be a connection between us as one and the same person.

Because the events of my life are far too numerous to relate at this time, I will continue to select a few examples and attempt to cover many aspects of the kind of occurrences that have dominated my life, in the hope that in the latter chapters of this book, when I reveal my findings you too will fully understand how I was to become so certain that at last I had found the undeniable truth. All the events I am about to relate did in fact take place during my life married to John and after having moved into my vision house.

So many times I would receive an urgent impulse to return home, or do something different from what I had planned to do, only to discover my assistance was needed in some way or other. I will give a few examples of these kind of incidents. The first one, however, does go back prior to the period I intend to speak of.

I gave birth to both of my children at home rather than in

our local hospital. After the birth of my first child I had not been out of the house for three weeks, so John suggested one day that he took care of the baby and I should visit my mother for a few hours. We had a lovely coal fire burning in the room where John sat, and the baby lay sound asleep in a little wicker basket crib in a small recess beside the chimney breast. After assuring myself that all was well I told John I would be back at 4 pm. Then I returned to the room and informed John that I wanted to place the crib in the bedroom instead of leaving it where it always had stood. He pointed out how cold the bedroom was, so having removed the crib I placed extra blankets over the baby. I arrived at my mother's house at about 1 pm. We sat drinking tea and at 1.45 pm when my mother asked if I would like another cup I felt panic rise inside me and said, 'No, I've got to get home.'

I thought the bus would never come and by the time it arrived I felt screwed up inside with this feeling of urgency. As I approached my home I understood why. Smoke was pouring out of our upper rooms where John and the baby were. I opened the door and looked up the stairs as John appeared at the top of them looking completely dazed. I ran upstairs and into the bedroom and grabbed the baby from her cot and took her to a neighbour's home. John had fallen asleep as soon as I had left and while he slept a large piece of coal had rolled off the fire and on to the pile of clean nappies I had placed beside the crib to air. The only part of the room damaged was in the recess where the baby's crib would have been.

It was a practice of mine to meet my mother each Wednesday at her local shopping centre. After shopping we would go to her house where I would stay until 3.30 pm. This we had done for over two years. When we had arrived at her home after having done our shopping on one of these occasions, once again I felt I had to return home, but did not know why as I felt no panic as I had on the previous occasion. I said, 'Mum, do you mind if I don't stay today?'

'Of course not,' she replied.

I returned home and remembered how when I was at my mother's home the thought of cleaning my car entered my head. This I could have done any time. I thought, 'Now that I am home I may as well clean the car.' I took two buckets out to the side of the house where my car stood, one with soapy water and the other for rinsing off the soap. I dipped into the soapy water and dropped the flannel into the clean water by mistake. I took the bucket back into the house to refill it with clean water and my phone rang. It was a woman sounding pretty anxious to know if I had the spare door key to the flat of a work colleague of hers who lived in a house we owned. I assured her I did have the key, and she asked if I would call on the woman and if I got no answer to use the key and see that she was all right. I did in fact have to use the key and found the young woman unconscious on the floor with an empty pill bottle beside her. I called back the caller as she had requested and then called the police, who in turn called an ambulance. The ambulance men said the woman was so near to death they dared not put her into the ambulance until they had brought her round a bit and walked her up and down the room until it was safe to take her to hospital. I can only assume that she had discussed suicide with her work colleague and when she failed to go to work on that particular day, the woman suspected the worst. When the woman came round she kept apologizing to me for what she had done in the house that John and I owned.

As I said, there is no way I can write all the events in the exact order that they occurred. So, bearing this in mind I would like to explain the circumstances surrounding how John and I purchased the property this young lady rented from us. Also note how two almost identical events take place as is usual with all my occurrences. I had long since had to include these points in my research.

I was cleaning my car at the side of my home when a young lady ran towards me from the opposite side of the road. She said, 'Would you please help me. I am a home help and have just discovered the elderly man I call on lying on the floor unconscious.' I went with her to a nearby house and as she had said he appeared to have had a heart attack. I dialled 999 from the house I was in and he was taken to hospital where we heard later that day that he had died. A few weeks later his house was put up for sale. John and I still wished to purchase a house but somehow after Ted had died we had not continued to look out for one. John now suggested we got the keys from the agent and looked at this one, as it was so near to home and also as it was in a bad state of repair the price would be reasonable. He also pointed out that most of the houses in this particular road were well maintained so this one was a good opportunity and should not be missed.

We obtained the keys and as we entered the house I said to John, 'We are never going to own this house and it is a waste of time looking at it.' John did not agree and continued to look the house over, but I returned home. The very next day John phoned the agent and made an offer on the house but was told it had been sold the day before. I assured John that something better would come along but he was very bitterly disappointed.

Two weeks later John asked if I would go to the builders' merchant the next day as he wanted a tin of special paint that he could only obtain there. The next day I got off the bus and walked towards the builders' merchant. I had to pass an estate agent and suddenly I had a very strong compulsion to go in. This was ridiculous as we could quite easily have contacted many estate agents in our search for a house had we desired to do so. I continued my journey to obtain the tin of paint. On my return journey, however, there was no way I could resist the impulse to enter the estate agent so this I did. 'Do you by any chance have any badly run-down properties for sale in this area?' I enquired.

'We did have,' the agent replied, 'but we have sold it.'

'Where was it?' I asked. It was, in fact, at the other end of the very road on which John had just lost the one he wished to buy. 'Has the exchange of contracts taken place?' I asked.

'No, but it is just the matter of the buyer getting a mortgage.'

'Then it is not sold,' I said. 'Take my name and phone number and if the buyer cannot get a mortgage then ring me.' This he did a week later and John and I purchased the house very cheaply because we agreed to allow the elderly lady who lived in the house to stay indefinitely. The home help for this elderly lady happened also to be the one who had asked for my assistance concerning the elderly man. They were the only two people cared for by this home help in this particular road, although other home helps worked in the vicinity and the same road.

You can see how one event after another include very small

details that do in fact connect each occurrence with the other? Over the course of the years many of my 'events' are joined in this way creating one long chain. Yet at the same time a different chain is also taking place. Once again I would like to point out that because of the nature of these events all can so easily be proven to be so.

I was next to discover that my thoughts could actually affect electrical and mechanical devices. Every time I mistakenly but briefly thought a piece of equipment had gone wrong but then discovered I had failed to switch it on or had pulled the plug partially out, within a week or sometimes within hours the mistaken belief became reality. The equipment would be truly broken. I could not accept this as a coincidence. Again, one day while I was cleaning and washing and idly thinking I asked myself how we would manage without electricity. Within seconds the whole circuit fused for no apparent reason.

John assured me that it was not overloaded and because the wiring had recently been renewed it was a mystery. I did not mention my thoughts at the time of it happening but knew I was the cause. I knew that I could not make these events happen at will. They occurred during a spell of day dreaming or followed on from everyday thoughts. I was always aware, however, that it was the very object I had previously been thinking about. Now I only think 'nice thoughts' about all electrical equipment.

I recall an instance when I was visiting a site where John and the men were working. When I arrived they all looked very fed up. It appeared that the large drill they had been using to remove an area of concrete had stopped working just as the job was almost completed. They had taken the drill to pieces twice but could find nothing wrong with it. To prove to me it would not work, one of the men tried it again. I said to him, 'Now stand over there and try it again.' I have no idea why I said this and in spite of the scorn on John's face, the man did as I said. The drill started up immediately and he removed the last piece of concrete.

Whilst taking my car to have the wheels balanced I watched as the lad removed a wheel and placed it on to a machine held on by a large wing nut. He then switched on the machine and rotated the wheel at a great speed. He then removed another wheel from my car and as he was securing the wheel to his machine I said, 'Aren't you afraid of that nut coming off while the wheel is spinning?'

He said, 'Well, it never has yet.' I moved to the side of his machine and as I did so the nut came off whilst the wheel was spinning. The lad in a panic switched off the machine and was desperately trying to slow the wheel down and hold it on the spindle at the same time. (Note: This event took place just a couple of years ago and could easily be verified.)

I now believe that events such as these had to take place as did many other kinds so that when I discovered the answer to my questions these were all to be used as examples. I had to be able to base everything on my own experiences. Anyone else's could be slightly exaggerated in the telling, or important details omitted.

Although there were other occasions that concerned electricity which helped to confirm my discovery that my thoughts did in fact affect such appliances, I will not at this time relate them. I would instead at this point like to return to other chains of events that were taking place in my life and start where I believe it began, although in my heart I am now fully aware they each undoubtedly began a long time before, but I do not recall when.

Although John and I had owned many cars I never once wished to learn to drive, but in 1970 I decided I would have lessons and obtain a driving licence. Somehow I thought it was something I was meant to do rather than a desire. I did pass on my first test and John bought me a cheap car to run around in. I had had this car for almost four years when I decided positively that I now wanted a really nice one that I would be proud to drive and call my own. I decided to use my old method and each night thought about a car. I felt it was a bit ambitious so to help it to materialize I entered as many competitions as possible in which a car was the prize.

John also had desires of his own. He wished desperately to have the willpower to give up smoking; he even paid a hypnotist to assist him. John also wanted to lose a good bit of weight and each evening would do exercises and push-ups in the hope of accomplishing this. John was forever asking me to purchase iron tablets that he felt sure he needed, or yeast tablets. I was against this and said his doctor would prescribe them if they were needed but John continued to take them. He also said how he so often dreamed of an early retirement to be able to do the things he would really like to do, rather then have all the worry of the company. I too was pretty fed up with being tied to our business now that the girls were grown up. All of our wishes were to be granted in just one day. John had a major heart attack at the age of forty-seven. On the hospital's advice and if he wished to live, he had to lose a lot of weight, stop smoking, take tablets, sell his company and go into early retirement. He did all of these things and gave me the brand new company car we had purchased which had been seldom used. I was free of the company to pursue my own desires.

A long time before all this took place I had become fully aware because of so many other incidents that when I wished for something I had to word it to myself very clearly and never allow for something bad to take place for my desire to materialize. Yet how innocent were these desires of John and myself and how serious the consequences.

Now that I was free of the company and could pursue my own interests, I decided I would like to do something on my own, but not go out to work and be in other peoples company each day. I did not know exactly what until one day when I was in conversation with a woman she happened to mention that a friend of hers who lived some thirty miles or so away sold a product from her home. I was very interested and asked her if she would give me her friend's telephone number, as I too would like to sell this product. Her friend was very helpful and explained that the supplier would only supply to one person in a radius of ten miles, and if there were no other agents in my area then he would supply me. There were no other agents and so I became the one for my area.

I had been an agent for about two years when I was quite shocked one day to see the very same product being delivered in bulk to a neighbour of mine just two houses away from my own. I contacted my supplier and asked how this was possible since I was the agent for this area. He too was puzzled and asked me the name of the people who lived in that particular house. I told him it was Tiller. 'Oh dear,' he said. 'Mr Tiller is the owner of the firm and lives in the north of England where this product is manufactured. The son of the owner of that house, however, is his nephew who is also a supplier for your area. He should in fact be your supplier and I am treading on his toes.' From that day on I was supplied by Mr Tiller Jr. His father, Mr Tiller, was none other than the man whose car refused to start outside our house, who had introduced John into factory maintenance and the company we formed. So Mr Tiller, our neighbour, had started us up in our first business many years previously, and his brother living as far away as the north of England had unknowingly done likewise for me in 1974.

John was not the sort of man who could sit around doing nothing, so even after he had sold the company he purchased a house to modernize in his own time, and when completed he sold it. It was soon after he had sold this property that I was to find that my mind was dominated by what I can only describe as a compulsive daydream. It was as though my mind had been invaded by alien thoughts over which I had no control. I tried desperately to rid my mind of these recurring thoughts yet still they returned. In this compulsive daydream there was always a large ship in the last stages of sinking. There were people in the water swimming and struggling, but away at the edge of the scene. I was only vaguely aware of these people and their plight. In the main part of this daydream there were two lifeboats, pulling away from the sinking ship in opposite directions. I was in one and as we moved apart I was able to see just two faces in the other lifeboat, even though it was close by and full of people. The two clear faces were of John and his cousin Ivy. The two lifeboats eventually drifted so far apart that the other one vanished completely from my view. Here the daydream would end, and begin all over again.

I could understand a recurring dream but not a recurring daydream. Had it not happened I would have said it was impossible. But the daydream continued for some months, much to my annoyance. One day I had a strange feeling that all was not quite right. John seemed on edge and not his usual self. That night he told me how he had purchased a large property at the coast very close to the home of his cousin Ivy, and would be spending a lot of his time there living and working on the property. He also said he intended to buy a small boat to go deep sea fishing in.

Now I understand my compulsive daydream which ceased

the moment John revealed his intentions to me. The months during which I experienced the daydream were in fact the months when John and cousin Ivy were negotiating the purchase of the property, and because contracts were to be exchanged the day after he finally told me, John knew he could no longer keep the truth from me.

We did, however, come to a very amicable arrangement and I fully understood that he had merely followed his doctor's advice to buy something at the coast and near to a relative if possible to escape the stress of living in London.

Now that we were each doing our own thing we were both very contented and had very much to talk about on the many visits John made home. The property he had purchased, however, was another matter, and although I had not seen it I felt sure that it was not one to spend a lot of money on. I advised John to separate the section he desired, and sell the remainder as it stood. This he agreed to do, but once he had completed the part he was to live in, he continued against my feelings to modernize the larger part also.

I, on the other hand, was very happy with the small part-time job I was doing, and set about re-decorating and refurnishing our home. So in my mind I could see that yet another kind of incident had to be added to my various events. Compulsive daydreams. At the time of experiencing the daydream it all appeared to be so foolish. Now, however, once John had revealed his secret intentions to me I realized it was very meaningful and obvious. And hadn't I also made contact once again via thought to create a new way of life for myself, now that the desire to be free of the company had become a reality.

I recalled at this time one of these occasions that had so recently taken place. John and I had company, and as we sat chatting, the wife said, 'Now that our children are grown up we would dearly love to see them marry so that Ian and I can be on our own.' Within six months their son had purchased a home of his own and the daughter had decided to share a flat with a friend. Only a matter of a couple of weeks after the daughter had moved out, Ian died at work of a heart attack. When I heard the sad news I thought 'If only Jill had said, "We would like it to be just the two of us now," instead of on our own,' which they most certainly were now.

In the course of my long research I found there were so many recurring details even though they seemed superficially so very unimportant, had to be included. All this merely added to the complexity of my research. Nothing seemed clear cut. As soon as I felt I had experienced everything, so a new kind of happening would occur, dispelling all the theories I had at that time arrived at. Deep down I knew that when I did have the evasive answers, each and every one of the mysteries surrounding my life would be resolved, in the very same way that John's heart attack caused a variety of wishes to be granted all at one time. It would account for everything. I felt that I had in my possession all the pieces of a giant jigsaw puzzle but could not lay them in the correct positions. I had an awareness that was not easy to fathom – that I already had all the answers inside me and that no book or person could ever show me this truth. I already knew it but could not recognize it.

I had heard how hypnotists were able to regress people and conceived the brilliant idea that I should be hypnotized to raise the answers to the surface. An appointment was made and I kept it in the pretence of wanting to be regressed, but really I was hoping for a miracle. It was a complete failure. Nevertheless, having met the hypnotist and having listened to all he had achieved with his regression sessions, I began thinking deeply about this subject, if only to come to terms in my mind with his claims. I also considered this to be an experience that I might at some later date wish to include as firsthand knowledge rather than hearing of regression via someone else. I have never considered anything that was to further my research a waste of time no matter how fruitless the results. If what I was searching for was to be easy, then I felt sure that someone else would have long since had the answers. My determination throughout my long search was strictly for my own benefit and satisfaction. I had long felt I did not have to prove anything, to anyone. Had I not spent most of my early life worrying what people thought, and ridiculed by those who thought themselves superior? I recall one such person who, having heard my views on this theme, had the audacity to say, 'Of course, if you had received the education I have had, you would not think as you do.' How correct he was; it is because I have used my own brain that I

70

am now in a position to write this book.

6

Back in my childhood, after the death of Billy Short, I made up my mind never to wish for anything again, but being a child and always wishing to be like the other children, when the skating fad died out, it was second-hand bikes that the children were buying. Those of us who had no bike, were naturally left out, as we had been without skates, but now we were left out of bike rides to places further afield. In spite of my vow, I began wishing once again. At that time I was twelve, my elder sister was coming up to her fourteenth birthday, and mum was looking on the boards where second-hand items were put up for sale, in the hope of buying her a second-hand sewing machine. Now although I was fully aware that mum was doing this I did not in any way think about the sewing machine, all I thought of was a bike.

At 5 pm one evening when all the shops were closing I stood in the doorway of our local bank. While standing there I felt a great determination to get the bike I so dearly wanted, so I repeated over and over again to myself, 'I am going to get a bike, I am going to get a bike. I am not leaving here until I get a bike.' I actually thought and believed that someone was going to come up to me and give me a bike. Still repeating the same words over and over again I stayed in that doorway for almost two hours. The large clock on the undertakers' opposite said it was 6.50 pm and I decided to go home.

I crossed the road and walked past the undertakers' still undeterred. At the second house I had to walk past a woman stood in her front garden. As I reached her she said to me, 'I have been clearing out my back garden shed, do you know anyone who would like this bike?' It was a girl's bike which she explained belonged to her daughter who was now serving in the Land Army. Then she added, 'I also have a Singer treadle sewing machine that I would sell for ten shillings.' So, once again I had obtained the very item I had so greatly desired. My mother bought the sewing machine for my sister and sold it to a rag-and-bone man some three years after the war for ten bob. Almost a year to the day after I got my bike it was stolen from outside the undertakers' while I was shopping.

I have related this event to point out that although my sister will well remember her birthday present, not she or anyone else would ever be able to conceive the turmoil in my mind that followed this apparently very ordinary event. Only I was aware of the whole story, and it was this awareness that was to cause so much stress in my life during childhood. However, as I grew older and had many more experiences of this nature behind me, the stress diminished to mere concern and a deep desire to search inwardly for the answer during quiet spells. Never once did this research become an obsession, since when each of the events took place it came after a very down-to-earth discussion or after having decided to do something along the lines of the events I have related in previous chapters. Even my nightly thoughts prior to an 'event' taking place invariably concerned what I intended to accomplish the next day; or if I had some sort of problem I would perhaps ask myself the best way to go about solving it. Now the reason I came to the conclusion that it was these thinking sessions before sleep that were the cause of these events taking place, was the fact that it was always after something I had thought about before sleep that the strange event occurred. After I had fully matured I simply accepted the situation, and if thinking on the subject I would calmly go over in my mind all that I could possibly recall about the various events and try to find something that would tie them all together.

I felt there was a very logical explanation that had no connection whatsoever with the claims of those people who dealt in spiritualism and who had so often tried to assure me that I had connections with spirits from the other side. I must admit, that at one time after having this kind of discussion, I did think it a possibility that the spirit of my sister Beth was still with me. Another conclusion I considered was the fact that as a very young baby I had been dropped on my head and I wondered if this had opened up a part of my brain that was closed to other people. Just like the times when we read of a blind person regaining their sight after a blow on the head. All this was merely speculation. My calm way of thinking continued for many years and then because of yet another event I became less indifferent and had to accept the fact that if I am responsible for all the good things that take place around me, then I must be responsible for the bad also, since nothing works one way only. These thoughts came to me in 1981 after the following event took place.

As was usual, on this particular Tuesday evening I went to my club where I met each week with three friends. That evening, however, only one of them turned up. Pat and I sat discussing her son's new baby and the fact that it was to be christened. She said she could not really make up her mind what to buy the baby for a christening present, but had seen something she might give. I asked what she had in mind, and she replied, 'It's a box with cellophane on the top and in it is a little silver eggcup and spoon.' I went cold from head to foot, recalling the death of my sister Beth, and said, 'Please don't buy it.' Pat asked why, and I told her about Beth and the silver eggcup and spoon and how she had died.

The next Tuesday Pat was not at the club and my two friends and I wondered why. The following Tuesday all three had already arrived when I got there. As I sat down Glad said to me, 'Pat has got some terrible news to tell you.' Pat then told me how on the morning of the previous Tuesday, her daughter-in-law Beth had discovered her baby was dead. A cot death the doctor said. Pat explained how the baby and Beth's other two-and-a-half year old daughter slept in an adjoining room. She checked on the baby at midnight, but in the morning it was dead. I was stunned and asked Pat if she had bought the eggcup and spoon after all, to which she said, 'Yes.'

How on earth could I possibly begin to understand this tragic event, and worse still, was I in some way responsible for having spoken of my sister's death to Pat? I went over all the similarities concerning the two deaths. The name of Beth, although uncommon, was involved. The circumstances also involved adjoining rooms, as I had mentioned when telling about Beth's death; the fact that I was two-and-a-half years old at the time and so was the sister of this baby. My sister Beth had been buried in her christening gown. This death too

74

concerned christening. And of course the eggcup and spoon. Why did I shudder? Did I recreate the event by speaking of it? These were the kind of questions I asked myself. Would it have happened if our other two friends had been there the week we sat and talked alone? How could I come to terms with this? And was I also responsible for Ted's death, and Billy Short's death? With these kinds of thoughts for a while I felt I could not handle the situation; but who on earth could I possibly discuss my problems with? Because of the frame of mind I was now in, I was filled with so many mixed emotions. And to make matters worse, all the strange events that had been taking place in my life were happening so fast and so continuously it was all so unbelievable. I became so very desperate that I phoned my doctor and made an appointment to see him. Once I had done this, however, all the stress suddenly left me and I became calm and collected. I cancelled the appointment and sat and laughed. I felt sure he would have had me put away once he heard my complaint.

I began to try to control my every thought. This helped to quite a degree, but it is obviously not possible to control all thoughts or to stop thinking. At least now I had the events happening at a pace which I could handle, and as all shocks or guilts that we may have about ourselves do gradually fade from our minds, so too did the feeling that I was responsible in any way for the deaths that had occurred.

As I have stated throughout, most of the events taking place were very down-to-earth, everyday happenings that on the surface seemed so natural. Yet they were more complex than they appeared, and had to be included in my search for the answers. I will now relate three instances involving telephone calls.

My mother was due to come out of hospital on a Friday having recovered from a minor complaint. On the evening of Thursday, the evening before she was due to go home, I passed the hospital in my car when suddenly it flashed across my mind 'Mum is dead.' I drove the short distance to my home and as I arrived my daughter came out of the house to inform me the hospital had just rung to say that Nan had died in her sleep. I replied, 'Yes, I know.'

On another occasion I was hoping that a builder had started carrying out some work on my behalf. I sat sewing, thinking idly about this when my phone rang and I was informed that it was in fact the builder speaking. He wished to contact the Building Inspector to discuss a query with him and wished to know if I could give him the Building Inspector's phone number. I took out a folder on which I had written the name of the inspector and his phone number. I gave the number to the caller and continued to sew. I then thought, 'As soon as I've finished this sewing I'll go to a Sainsbury's store in the hope that they could help me with a problem I had.' My thoughts were interrupted by the phone ringing again. It was the same builder who had just rung me. He asked, 'What was the number you gave to me?'

I picked up the folder from the table and repeated what was written, having phoned this man many times myself. I said, 'Mr Coombe,' and repeated the telephone number.

'That's right,' the man replied. 'That's the same number I rang. I asked the receptionist to be put through to Mr Coombe's office, which she did, but it was a Mr Coombe from Sainsbury's store.' Yes, another branch of the very store I intended to visit.

At 3.30 pm one day I received a phone call informing me that a relative of mine had died, with a request to make all the necessary arrangements for his burial. I was the only relative the hospital could contact should anything happen to him. Because of the time of day, I could not notify other members of my family as they were working. I contacted them later. The call notifying me of his death came from his social worker. Prior to my uncle's death he had asked me to give his watch to a particular tradesman who had been kind to him. But because my uncle had lived some distance from my home there was no way I could locate this man, or even be sure it was the man he meant. So I gave the watch to another member of my family who had been a favourite of my uncle. Some four years later the relative I had given the watch to, called me for the first time since receiving it, and naturally, recalling that I had not complied with my uncle's wishes, a pang of guilt went through me. It was nearly three-thirty when the relative arrived at my home and almost immediately my phone rang. I answered it and could not believe what I was hearing. It was an almost identical conversation to the one that took place when the social worker informed me of my uncle's death. For a second or two I

76

thought she was going to tell me he had died again, but it turned out that she was calling to ask if he would return some crutches he had borrowed some years previously. I assured her that my uncle had never borrowed crutches, and that he had died three or four years ago, and it was her office that had informed me. She apologized and said she didn't really know why she had bothered me as the missing crutches were very old anyway. Could it be? I wondered. I sorted out the death certificate and, yes, my uncle had died four years ago that very day, and I had been notified of his death at exactly the same time as this call.

Some years ago I had been waiting several months to hear from a particular government office. I said to John, 'I am fed up with waiting, so I am going to ring them.' He said it was better to wait to hear from them as it would put me at a disadvantage if they thought I was too keen for their reply. I said, 'Nevertheless, I am going to have a cup of tea and then contact them.' Having drunk my tea I was walking towards the telephone when it rang. Yes, it was the office I intended contacting, ringing to apologize for having kept me waiting so long for their reply, which was good news.

Providing it was vital that I needed to contact someone, and I had no way of doing so, I would merely keep saying over in my mind, 'Ring me ----' and more often than not they did. And when I would ask why they had rung at that particular time, invariably they said it was on impulse.

Over a period of years I had several dreams which, when I awoke, I knew were not of the normal kind. So much so that I made it a practice to tell them to someone, so that at a later date when their meaning became obvious it could be verified that I did in fact dream before the event and not after.

In the first of these dreams I was standing halfway up a hill overlooking a pretty sunlit market square. The sun was not as we know it: the rays I felt were pure and pleasant, giving a feeling of wellbeing. There were about thirty people in various parts of the square, some in pairs, some walking alone. All were smiling as though it was a very happy occasion and as if they all shared something special. From where I stood, although at some distance, I could see none of them were speaking and yet they were obviously conversing. I then realized that I recognized them all as people I had known who had died. This dream remained vividly when I woke up, and I felt the people in my dream had been trying to tell me something which I could not grasp.

Another dream I had was short and urgent. In this dream, I was in bed when a nun appeared beside my husband who was lying asleep beside me. She appeared to be floating rather than standing and was looking across my husband towards me. She pointed her finger slowly at me and said, calling me by my full Christian name, which no one ever did, 'Take care of the baby,' and she was gone. I awoke, startled by the exactness of this dream and the name Theresa dominated my mind. I lay thinking about the dream and decided that the nun must have been Saint Theresa. I looked at the clock and saw it was 3 am. The next day I told John about my dream and then forgot it until 3 am the following morning when John and I were awakened by the telephone ringing. It was a close friend of ours to say she had had a terrible row with her husband and he was in their flat with the baby and he had thrown her out in her night clothes. She asked if John would drive round and pick her up. She was afraid for her baby, but the following day John took her home to get the baby. I cared for the baby while she looked for somewhere to live. The baby's name was Theresa.

Some months before the following dream my mother had been told that she must have a cataract operation on her eye. She was very afraid and said how she dreaded hearing from the hospital. I asked her when it would be done, and she said because so many people required this particular operation the hospital had been unable to say. They informed her that it could be a month or even many months before she was sent for. My next abnormal dream concerned this letter she was awaiting. In my dream I had called on my mother and as I entered her front door, I picked a letter from the mat. It was a long brown envelope and when my mother opened it, it contained a small white slip. While she was reading the slip I thought, 'How silly, that could have been sent in a small envelope.' My mother said, 'I have got to go in for my eye operation on the 7th January.' I then awoke. I told John my dream and since the 7th January was some six weeks away, he told me to write the date of my dream on the back of our calendar. This I did and when visiting my mother I told her about my dream. I completely forgot the incident until the end of December when I went to visit my mother, She looked very concerned and I enquired what was wrong. She said, 'It has come.' I asked, 'What has come?' She said, 'The long brown envelope with the little white slip informing me that I shall have my operation on the 7th January.'

There were other dreams which were to stay in my mind and to which I gave much thought although they were of a different kind. In one such dream I was a student in a hospital and sat among other students, listening to a doctor lecturing on medical matters. Although I could not repeat the lecture because of the medical terms used, I was fascinated by the knowledge being passed to us, the students. This dream intrigued me, especially as I had no medical knowledge of the kind being given in the lecture. Yet this was my dream and came from my subconscious. How could this be?

A second dream made me feel the same. Throughout the entire dream I was quoting aloud a beautifully wordèd poem as I witnessed all that had inspired it. I stood beside a white-haired old woman at the gate of her isolated cottage and watched a battle going on, while quoting all I saw in verse. This was an olden day battle and the soldiers wore dusty torn uniforms like those in the 16th century. Did this also come from within me? There were so many things and situations to consider when searching for the elusive answers.

One of the most surprising events to take place happened on just one occasion.

John and I had had an extremely busy day and we were exhausted as we prepared to call it a day. I sat idly day-dreaming and was thinking about having been told a few days previously about people being able to leave their bodies. I had been visited by three members of a research organization that investigated events such as these I experienced. It was they who had informed me that it is a known fact that many people have claimed that their spirits have left their bodies. It was this conversation my mind dwelt on, and I thought, 'Could a person really leave his body?' Then I became aware that John had spoken. In spite of having heard what he said, I drearily said, 'What did you say?'

To which he replied, 'Can a person really leave their body?'

There was stunned silence for a moment and I said, 'What did you say?'

In quite an alarmed voice he said, 'I know what I said. I heard myself say it, but don't know why.' This was indeed a completely new experience and even though John was deeply concerned by what had taken place, I knew that I dared not tell him that he had spoken my thoughts. I had by this time concluded he was a little afraid of my abilities and this was why he did not care to discuss them. If he imagined that by pretending they did not really happen, they would not be there any more, he must have long since realized that this was not to be so.

Then right out of the blue, John would suddenly surprise me and openly ask me to use my ability to assist him in some way. Once I had done as he requested he no longer wished to discuss the affair.

One of the occasions when John sought my help was after he had seriously hurt his back and was in great pain, hardly able to move. When this happened in the past he had had to consult an osteopath, where he went for many visits before being cured. On about the third day of seeing him in pain and frustrated at sitting in a chair all day, I thought to myself, 'I wonder if I could cure him?'

Within five minutes he said to me, 'I was just thinking. I wonder if you could cure me?' I had twice in the past accomplished such cures so I agreed to try, and told him to lie on the floor and I would gently massage where the pain was. With great difficulty he did as I asked, and with a little oil on my hands to prevent friction I gently moved my hands over the painful part of his back. After just two or three minutes I told him to stand up and see how it felt. He got up quite easily and declared that his back was now OK except for just a slight twinge. He also said how very hot my hands were, which I presumed was caused by the oil.

The second occasion John had cause to ask for my help was when he phoned me from the coast and was obviously greatly distressed. All the symptoms of a previous serious infection had returned after many years, and he feared he would have to undergo a similar operation as was carried out on the first occasion. He had seen two doctors, taken many types of antibiotics, had hospital tests and still they could find no reason for his condition, so it was suggested that he returned to hospital on his next visit to London if the prescription he was then taking had no effect. He told me that he was worse than ever and was so scared that in spite of always having claimed to be an atheist, he had been praying. I simply told him to take a tranquilizer, go to bed and when he woke up he would feel 99 per cent better. I was awakened at 7 am the next day by the ringing of the telephone. John said, 'I can hardly believe it. I feel marvellous.' Yet when he paid his next visit to London not one word was ever mentioned about the incident.

Having asked myself so many times over the years, 'Why me?' I made many mental notes about myself and felt it a possibility that a combination of them all may well have some bearing on the answer to this question. I concluded that my brain, unlike other people's, was more or less filled with my own thoughts and not those received from religion, books and education. Also, as I have a very good memory, I decided that this too could contribute to the very clear way I can visualize things, so much more clearly than a learned person. I feel that if I had been highly educated I most certainly would not have had a clear picture of the many and varied events which led me to write this account. It would have created too much conflict within me. During my life I thought of many various explanations only to be forced to discount them at a later date.

There were times, working long hours with John, when I became aware of being very tensed up inside. Thoughts would come to me which were so alien that I would push them from my mind. I would get irritable for no apparent reason, and the moment John departed from my company I would feel my true self again. There were also very many times when I would be thinking of either doing something, or purchasing something, and almost immediately John would either ask me to do the very thing I had just made up my mind to do, or would mention the very item I had been considering purchasing. Invariably although he referred to the same item, it would be in connection with his work or something he felt he would like to take to his Mother on his next visit. Because this happened on far too many occasions to be considered merely coincidence, I began to wonder if somehow our minds had joined forces and if this was the reason we were able to make such a success of the company and achieve the impossible. Or, I wondered, did he also have the ability to demand the things he wanted? I recalled too that many of the things he longed for or desperately needed often materialized after he, rather than I, had met the individual possessing the object, although I had been working on obtaining it. Could it be that I was demanding the item to appear directly for John rather than via me to avoid embarrassment? I did not know the answer to these questions.

When John went to live at the coast I decided that now was the chance to see what would transpire when we were living far apart and completely unaware of each other's daily actions and desires. Nothing had altered. During the many phone calls that were to take place between us I was to discover that on many occasions John had either carried out the same task as I had, or had been involved with a very similar conversation as I too had had here at home. On one particular occasion John actually openly asked me about my recent thoughts as he felt sure that I was connected with something that had happened to him at the coast. He asked if I had been thinking about a round table. That very morning I had awakened with the determination that I would not have yet another square coffee table in my newly decorated and furnished front room. I would go out that very day and buy a round one. I went to every store I could possibly think of in the hope of finding the round coffee table I wanted so much, but without any success. I had no choice but to settle for a square one, because I wanted John to see the room completely finished when he came home as he had planned to do on the following Tuesday. The day of my purchase being a Friday I asked that the coffee table be delivered first thing on Monday. I told John all these facts and he then told me why he had cause to ask such a question. He said, many times friends of his at the coast had invited him to their home for a meal, and he had always been in a position where he was unable to accept. That day, however, he was invited to a midday meal with them. He explained that after the meal, just he remained at the table while the others sat in armchairs in the room chatting. He said he had his elbow lightly resting on the large round table when for no apparent reason the thick leg of the table split from top to bottom and crockery fell to the floor.

On the Monday morning my coffee table was duly delivered and as the man was about to leave I pointed out that there were scratch marks on the table. Because it was the only table of its kind in stock I agreed to have a french polisher call that afternoon to attend to these marks. When the man arrived he looked at the marks and said, 'You had no need to send for me, your husband could have done this.'

I replied, 'Apart from the fact I have just paid quite a sum of money for this table, and it should be in perfect condition, my husband is away at the coast.' The moment I had said it I realized that this was not the kind of man you informed you were without a man in the house, so I quickly added on impulse. 'His father has been taken very ill, and he will be home later this evening.' That evening John telephoned me to say that he would not be home the next day as planned, as his father had been taken very ill.

His father is never ill, and even today at the age of eighty-seven he is still very active and only in recent years did he decide not to drive his car any more.

Since nothing had altered with distance between us, what was I to think? I did, however, realize why John had a heart attack at such an early age. Whereas I could look on setbacks as another of life's challenges, John would take a very negative attitude and work himself up to a terrible degree over even the smallest of daily annoyances. I had then become so anxious to see that all ran smoothly to avoid his reactions that now he was away from home I actually became a different person. He, however, still had the same aggravations at the coast as those he had hoped to escape from in London. During his visits home I would again become tensed up just listening to all that he had to cope with. Once he returned to the coast, all would be so calm again that the calmness almost shouted at me. For the first time in the whole of our married life I realized just how different our dispositions were. When we were living together prior to John going to the coast all our desires and activities were so combined there had been no way for this to become apparent.

I feel it appropriate at this time to include the contents of a report which was made by two of the three members of a local psychic research organization after they requested a meeting with me.

REPORT ON EVENING SPENT WITH MRS B. –
FRIDAY, FEB 15/80
THREE MEMBERS PRESENT, 7.30 – 10.15 pm

After preliminary introductions and an assurance from me that we were genuinely interested in what she experienced, together with a promise we would not divulge family confidentiality, Mrs B. talked freely and frankly, with little prompting. She is a married lady with two grown-up daughters – she has a comfortable home. Mrs B. said she doesn't read much but as she talked it was obvious she had reached a number of conclusions which echo some of the thinking of current researchers. The main point made by Mrs B. was that she believed in 'the power of the human brain'. She was brought up a Catholic but doesn't believe in religion although she has an open mind and respects people's right to believe if they wish. She said she rarely discussed, even within her own family, the 'experiences'.

She became aware, at an early age, of an ability to influence events and 'read minds'. As a child (and a member of a large family) she liked being on her own but *never felt she was alone*. She has had pre-cognitive thought but the main element is her conviction to 'always get what I want'. Numerous examples of this were given, including some startling facts about the way her husband's business had built up and now the family assets, Over the years Mrs B. has been able to win sums of money by backing winners – and has travelled widely – including the Near and Far East and Canada all of which she says she willed to happen.

Note: Examples given at this stage are included in previous chapters of this manuscript.

So far we have

   (i) willing events
   (ii) precognition
   (iii) faith healing and
   (iv) unpredictable means to achieve the end desire.

More examples are given at this point.
We then shifted discussion to Mrs B's view of what it was all

about. She advanced some conclusions she had arrived at which were quite startling given that, as she said, she rarely reads books.

1. That 'we are all made of electricity and out in space there's a mass which I can tune into'.
2. That we 'hang on to life desperately when we're here – but after death we go back into the mass'.
3. The Earth has been visited in the past by beings from elsewhere – but 'in the past the water was where the land is and the land is where the water was, so all the evidence is hidden from us'.
4. She knows about the Bloxham Tapes and asked, 'Why can't we send someone forward beyond their death?'
5. On regression hypnosis she advanced her idea of 'inherited' or 'genetic' memory.
6. 'I feel part of something – we are not alone'.

We then went back over some of her experiences.

We then asked if she had any recurring dreams – and yes, she had.

It was visiting a large house but always in the house there was a new room to go into. 'I feel as if I'm on a visit – perhaps visiting – is that possible? – could I be a sort of ghost for other people?'

A few other pieces of information, held for the end.

1. Mrs B. stated she 'always performs better when she doesn't eat'.
2. She was dropped on her head when a baby and had a blood clot removed – 'could this have made me the way I am?'
3. She knows which side of her brain is thinking – the right side is the one she uses for 'getting things done' whilst the left hand side deals with 'ordinary, every day things'. She sleeps on her right hand side when she wants something done.

She said she had no incentive to do much more as she had all she wanted – she didn't want publicity as people didn't understand or made fun but she was interested to hear of other people who shared her kinds of experiences.

I suggested that she might like to try to use her powers to

help others as she had now virtually achieved her own needs. She took on this idea –. there's a little boy with leukaemia whom she knows – he has only a few weeks to live. She is going to try to help him – and will let us know if it works.

She is going to see if she can 'pick up' some advanced information of major happenings – most recently when thinking about the coal strikes and the closing of coalmines she had an image of them all 'farming the waste tips and slag heaps' – she may be right in a few years' time.

I suggested that she might keep a diary – she wants to know of others who have similar experiences to hers.

So – a convincing evening covering a variety of experiences – we were made very welcome and thanked Mrs B. for her time and hospitality.

We agreed to keep in touch.

R.W.P.

POSTSCRIPT. Since writing the foregoing we received a call from Mrs B. on Tuesday 19th Feb, taken by my wife – her account now follows.

Mrs B. could not recall whether she had told us on the previous Friday evening (in fact she hadn't) that she sent a cheque on the preceding Wednesday to the parents of the boy with leukaemia. Although she had been thinking about him ever since their meeting three weeks before, he seemed particularly in her mind last week and she wrote telling his parents to buy him whatever he wanted to make him happy in his remaining time.

On Tuesday morning she had a phone call from the boy's mother, telling her the boy had died (three weeks earlier than predicted by the doctor) last Friday afternoon (ie. he was already dead when Mrs B. spoke to us).

Her cheque had arrived that Friday morning and to the boy's mother the thing he seemed most to want was to have his father with him. He had already asked his father to stay home from work but this would have involved loss of pay and was not financially possible. On receiving the cheque, the boy's mother rang his father at work to tell him he could now afford to take time off to be with his son.

He returned home at once. The boy died later that day with

his father at his side.

J.P. 19/2/80

7

The movement of objects in my home began back in 1967, after the sudden death of a close friend of ours. This friend owned an electrical shop and it was he who had sold John the radio that I was given for my birthday. About a day or so after his funeral had taken place, John got up first, as was usual, at 6.30 am and was amazed to find the radio on the floor in the centre of the room when it usually stood on the shelf. We could only assume that one or other of the girls had been sleep-walking and placed the radio there, since if obviously had not fallen. The next morning, however, it was once again in the middle of the room. Still we put it down to one of the girls sleep-walking and forgot all about the incident, until 1972 when John's mother died very unexpectedly of a heart attack.

About six months later I had spent all one day cutting flowers from the front garden to decorate the sideboard in the front room, which I had polished and cleaned in readiness for my in-laws to visit that evening. I had an appointment and could not be there when they were due to call. While I was at my appointment that evening I was daydreaming and began imagining where each of John's family would be sitting in my front room at that moment. I thought, 'His father will be in an armchair, John will be sitting in the other one facing him, and his cousin Ivy, her husband and his mother will be seated on the settee. No,' I thought again, 'His mother is dead.' The sudden realization of my thought jolted me and I looked at the clock. I noted it was 9 pm and thought they would have gone before I returned home. When I arrived home I asked John how the evening had gone and he said, 'A very strange thing happened here this evening.' I said to him 'I bet it happened at 9 pm.' He agreed that it did and went on to explain that someone had remarked that it was 9 pm, and as they did so a flower from the vase that I had placed on the sideboard for no apparent reason had sprung out from among the others and had landed in the middle of the room.

The third occasions occurred after the death of my uncle. A week or so after his funeral had taken place, John had found milk from the refrigerator in the middle of the floor. Recalling all three incidents after this third event I could not help but realize that each of the items concerned with each of these three deaths did in fact have an association with the person who had died. The radio was obvious in the first case. John never visited his mother without having stopped on the way to buy flowers for her. When John and I visited my uncle prior to his illness, we always refused a second cup of tea, being fully aware that if we did so we would leave him very short of milk. Still, however, always looking for a logical answer I thought it a possibility that on each of these occasions it may have been either John or I who had been sleep-walking and moved the radio and the milk, and the flower incident was nothing more than a coincidence. Then yet another object was found moved from its rightful place and this time I could find no logical explanation.

On one of John's visits to his doctor while he was in London, I went with him and we were in the doctor's waiting room when I saw John was reading a plaque on the wall. I too went across the room and saw it was headed 'Go Silently Through Life'. I said to John, 'That is the same as the one I have in the hallway at home that is called "The Desiderata".' John said that he did not think this was so and said how lovely the words were. When we arrived home, I pointed out to John my plaque and he agreed that it was in fact the same wording as the one he had read at the doctor's. He spent a period of time in London and then returned to the coast. A short time later a relative of mine informed me that she was to attend the funeral of a young woman who had tragically died of cancer. On the night before the funeral I had been in bed some three hours or so and had awoken thirsty, so I decided to get up and make myself a cup of tea. It was about 2.30 am. Having made the tea I returned to the bedroom where I lay thinking for half an hour or so. I then got up to go to the bathroom and went into the hallway once again. I was shocked to find that in the space of half an hour, the plaque was no longer on the wall where it had been firmly fixed, but now stood upright against the wall around the corner in such a position that had it been there when I made the tea there was no way that I could not have seen it, or have either knocked it over, or had to step over it. Now for the first time I did connect each of these events as something more than coincidence. Only a couple of nights before this event, I had decided I would take the plaque down and read the words. The day after this event when talking to John on the phone, I told him what had taken place and he said, 'You are not going to believe me but this is the gospel truth. Last night in bed I thought to myself, when I get home I am going to read the words on the plaque again.' So I felt I had yet another kind of experience to add to my collection.

During the first year of John living between the coast and London, one of my daughters had married and was now living a short distance away. The other daughter was still at home and was in regular employment, and I continued selling the product I mentioned in an earlier chapter. And as I have already stated, many varied chains of events were taking place in my life at one and the same time. I would now like to relate one that I can only assume began at the point where I shall begin. It may, however, have begun several years before this, when I had the dream about the operation my mother had for cataract, or maybe it began in John's family.

Back in 1979 I was supposed to help prepare food for an evening get together, but that weekend I developed a very bad cold and decided to use Contac pills to hold it off until after the weekend. Having taken these in the past I was aware that they make your eyes sore, because they seem to dry them at the same time as drying up your cold. On the Sunday my eye was beginning to irritate and I thought that I had better not rub it as it would become bloodshot. That evening I had an unexpected call from John to say how worried he was as he had just looked in the mirror and discovered that his eye was completely bloodshot, and this had happened to his mother on the day she had her fatal heart attack. I asked if there was any way he could get hold of the doctor he used when at the coast, but he assured me that this would be impossible on a Sunday. I then suggested that I contact his doctor here on the emergency number he had given us, and I would ring John back with his instructions. The doctor assured me that there was nothing for John to worry about and told me to tell him to take a tranquilizer and relax, and if he was coming to London in the near future to make an appointment. I phoned John with these instructions and John was very relieved. He then told me what had taken place while he was waiting for this phone call from me. The bell rang, and being a cold dark night he wondered who it could be. It was the doctor's wife out canvassing. So while I was speaking to his doctor here in London, he too was being assured by the doctor's wife at the coast that there was no cause for alarm, and then she was joined at his door by her husband who was also canvassing.

When John came home on his next visit he greatly admired the way I had redecorated the bedroom and said how nice the bed looked in the bay. He said, 'We used to have it there before, why did we move it out?' He then added, 'I know, it was in case the window was ever smashed when we were in bed.' I did not reply but thought to myself, 'Yes, you believe that was the reason,' knowing full well that we had to remove it because John had complained of back ache due to the draught from the windows, and if I were to remind him of this he would again complain of back ache.

He had been back at the coast only a week or so when one night in the early hours of the morning I was awakened by some kind of disturbance going on outside my house. I jumped out of bed and looked out of the window, and at that very moment a bottle smashed the window in my face. The glass damaged my eye and I had to undergo an operation. There were also many splinters of glass in my forehead. My daughter arranged for a friend to stay with her while I was in hospital the night following the accident, and she also told her employer what had happened. I only stayed in hospital for one night and the evening I came home my daughter received a phone call from the friend who had stayed with her the previous night. This friend said that she was on her way to hospital as she had had an accident and had a piece of glass in her eye. The policeman who came after my accident had called at my home on four occasions needing information from me. But each time he called I was at the hospital for dressings, so he asked my daughter if I would call at the police station and leave the information he required with the duty desk officer. I did this on the Friday and the young policeman asked what had happened. I told him the details, and he said he would pass the message on to the policeman dealing with my case. The next day a very bad accident occurred at the police station and a young policeman suffered a serious eye injury. When a photograph of him appeared in our local paper, although I could not be 100 per cent sure, it most certainly looked like the very one I had spoken to. The week following this incident, my daughter's employer had developed a very sore eye and had gone to her doctor. That weekend she was in so much pain that her husband took her to the hospital where they transferred her to the eye hospital I had so recently been in. It was discovered that the poison from her eye had gone into her bloodstream and she had two eye operations before being sent home.

Because the chain was so obvious I spoke of it to a young girl I knew. An hour after leaving her I met her again and she was holding her hand over her eye. She said, 'You and your eye chain, a tractor has just driven past me and thrown grit into my eye.' Later that week I was to meet her boyfriend, and he told me how she had told him all that had taken place, and the following day he had got sawdust in his eye in the butcher's shop where he worked and had to go to the chemist and get it removed by the pharmacist.

At this time I had been feeling rather guilty for not having called on a sister of mine, although we were in touch by phone and she was well aware of my accident. I told her on the phone that I would call on her the next morning as I had to pass her house. When she opened the door I saw she had a black eye and asked her how she had done it. She said, 'There was nothing wrong with my eye when I went to bed last night and this is how it was this morning.'

For some three months it appeared that the eye chain had at last gone away until one day I met with a friend at my club whom I had not seen since the eye incident. She asked how my eye was now, and I assured her it was all right and went to buy teas. When I returned I noticed her eye was bloodshot and asked what was wrong with it. She replied, 'There was nothing wrong with my eye until I met you.' Now this woman was unaware of anything other than my own injury so really had no reason to make this remark.

A few months after my accident I found pieces of glass that had been buried in my forehead coming to the surface of the small scars that had healed. Much more recently, April 1986, I discovered after all this time yet another of these splinters of glass had emerged through the scar. I naturally recalled the original accident. The very next night I again heard a disturbance outside our usually quiet road and jumped out of bed to investigate; but this time I ran and opened the front door, and hit the side of my eye on the edge of the door. At this moment of writing I have the last yellow marks of the back eye I have been sporting. During this period I heard that John's cousin Ivy has a very serious eye complaint which means she will be under hospital treatment for the rest of her life. This is why I said at the beginning of this chain of 'eye' events, 'Did it begin in John's family?'

Because I disliked cousin Ivy so much, during the five years John was to spend living between the coast and London I visited his coastal home only about four or five times and even then never stayed overnight. John had, against my advice, spent a lot of money on the larger part of the property and now the work was nearing completion he hoped to sell it all up and return to London, The 1st March 1981 was a Sunday and throughout the entire day I felt an urgent impulse to write down accounts of certain periods of our married life together which included many of the strange events. So compulsive were these thoughts that on the Monday as soon as I was alone I took out my typewriter and typed almost automatically, every spare moment I had, until the 25th of the month when I knew I had completed what I was meant to do.

I could only assume that these writings were intended for a member of a society I had recently come into contact with, that investigated events which appear to have no logical explanation. So I gave the copy I had made to this society and over the next year it was forgotten. John, who by now had reached the very last stage of completing the work at the coast made an arrangement to meet a would-be buyer and said he would return to London on Tuesday 2nd March 1982.

On Monday 1st March 1982 at about 4.30 pm I was driving along the road heading home when I saw a policeman strolling along. I thought 'How unusual seeing a policeman in this road,' then on the spur of the moment I pulled up and asked his advice about a car that a tenant of ours had left after having moved away which was in a dangerous condition. He said he would call at my home and collect the address of the owners and make them remove it. I drove home and sought out the address ready to give it to the policeman. He called about ten minutes later and after having given him the address I asked if he would like a cup of tea. I had made a pot of tea for my daughter and myself, so I poured three cups and we joined my daughter in the front room. Within five minutes my telephone rang, and my daughter went into the hall to answer it. It was cousin Ivy with the sad news that John had just had a fatal heart attack and his body had been taken to the mortuary. The policeman promptly took over the situation and made contact with relatives and advised us not to leave for the coast until the following morning. Later our family were amazed that I should have a policeman in my home at such a time as this.

John had died exactly one year to the day when I had received the compulsive thoughts to write down certain events. For the first time in eighteen years I was to meet cousin Ivy. The only thing I am prepared to state about all that took place after John's funeral is that all that I had written the year previously was vital to me and not intended for the people to whom I had given the copy, but cousin Ivy and her family.

Now I was faced with the problem of selling the property I had so strongly advised John not to spend money on, as from the onset, when he purchased this property I felt something was very wrong. It was valued for probate purposes and although it looked beautiful after all the work John had carried out, every would-be buyer withdrew their interest after a surveyor's report. This property caused me great concern over the following two years so when someone made an outrageously low offer for it I gladly accepted it. This was in June 1984. Having signed the contract and returned it to the solicitor I went away on a week's holiday for the first time in many years. I went at the request of a young relative who wanted me to go with her. We went to the Portsmouth area by the coast on 9th June. I knew that on my return the property would no longer be mine. I would still very much have liked to

94

know what was wrong with it, now I felt relieved that it was no longer my concern. To me the whole place looked beautiful after all the work John had carried out, but I always felt something was very wrong with it. I did not, however, have the time or the inclination to go to the coast to investigate. I simply loathed the place and wished only to be rid of it.

On Monday 11th June, in a crowded ballroom I met an elderly couple who struck me immediately as out of place, more the type of people to go to a private hotel for their holidays. However, we became friendly and met again in the ballroom the next evening. I asked where they came from, and the man said that they lived some fifty miles away in a coastal area and named it. I was amazed as this was the very place where John had died. I asked if he knew the road in which John had lived and he said, 'I most certainly do, I owned number eighteen for over twenty years and sold it to a builder called John five years ago.'

I said, 'I am John's widow.' He then told me that after John had died and the property was not sold, he had constantly wondered what was happening about it. I told him of all the difficulties I had trying to sell it and he agreed I had done the right thing in selling cheaply because the property was damp throughout and nothing would rid the place of this dampness. It seeped up through the walls no matter how much money was spent in the attempt to cure it. Now I understand why the wallpaper that John had so recently put on was coming away from the walls in various parts of the building. I had thought at the time of seeing this that the newly plastered walls had not sufficiently dried out before John had papered them. And could this be the reason John had cause to re-plaster so many walls in the building? John had said so many times that he was fighting a losing battle. So now, just what were the chances of my meeting the previous owner in this way?

During the months that followed John's death I spent time at the coast seeing various people and finalizing the last of the work on the property. Ivy and her family very kindly accommodated me on these occasions, and now that I had got to know Ivy I discovered she was the first person I had ever met in the whole of my life that I could relate the whole of my strange life to. In the years that followed, without Ivy's understanding and encouragement, I would never have dared even to consider the writing of this book. With her approval I also contacted a husband and wife who had come into my life briefly some time back in 1981. We four alone were the only ones with any knowledge of this manuscript for a long time. Ivy, in the short time I have really known her, has witnessed many of the strange events taking place in my life. She too understands the importance of what I am now in a position to reveal for further investigation by those more capable than myself. It is something I have to do. There is, however, much more that I am able to say on the subject that I do not have the ability to include in this book.

8

In 1983, after the many changes and adjustments that had to be made to my life now that John had passed away and my second daughter had moved into a place of her own, I was to experience yet another recurring daydream, which came to dominate my mind as the previous one had done. Now, however, I was convinced that that one had been very meaningful and could only wonder on this occasion why the daydream was so foolish. As with the previous one, I desperately tried to eliminate it from my mind, but with no success. While I was getting this daydream I confided in cousin Ivy, having already told her about the previous one. In this new daydream I was fourteen, and because of many false accusations made by various members of my family about things I had not done, I had gone to America. But even with strangers it appeared I was to be falsely accused. There was just one couple, a husband and wife that I would talk to and they usually came to me when I was seated under a large tree in the far side of a field. The strange thing about this daydream was, that although it was warm and sunny when I sat under the tree, in my mind it was in fact Christmas time. My feelings inside when alone under that tree were that I knew quite a lot about life but did not wish to tell anyone what I knew. Only my christian name I made known. If I did not fall asleep before this point, I was unable to proceed any further with the scene and would start again at the beginning. This went on for several months and suddenly ceased.

During the latter part of 1983, it all began to materialize. The most absurd accusations were made against me by even the closest members of my family. So outraged was I that I wanted nothing whatsoever to do with any of them. One person actually claimed that I had been having an affair with the policeman who happened to be at my home on the day I received news of John's death. It was all so unbelievable, but continued into 1984. And try as I would to ignore the whole affair, more and more accusations followed. At the end of February 1984 I felt so very, very angry about the whole affair that night after night I demanded in my mind to know what exactly it was all about. Just as I had done so on many other occasions in my life when I desperately required something. Having followed this procedure for a week or two, I then ceased to demand to know the answers because there were so many much more important things to think about concerning what was taking place.

To occupy myself I decided to redecorate the whole of my living quarters, even though I had already redecorated the hall and breakfast room a short time earlier, just after John had died. I did not like the paper I had chosen so I decided to renew it, and also redecorate my bedroom. Having completely made up my mind that these were the areas I would concentrate on, I first set about looking for a wallpaper I would like to have in these rooms. Then, because of a burst water tank, each of the very rooms I had decided to work on was very badly damaged. My insurance company promptly paid out on the damage to these rooms. None of the parts of the house that I had not decided to redecorate were affected in any way. So you see just how, in a very down-to-earth way, all my desires were to be granted, and yet from a very ordinary way of thinking.

After John had died I had wondered if all these events would cease, because so many of the ones in the past had concerned John. Now, however, I was to realize this was not to be the case. In the early part of September 1984, as it was a lovely day, I decided to wash and polish my car inside and out. This I did and then stood back to admire it, the very same car that John had given to me after his first heart attack. I had taken great care of it throughout the years, and in spite of having had it stolen on two occasions, under unusual circumstances, I had got it back each time. On the first of these occasions I had left my car one afternoon to go shopping. When I returned and found it had been stolen I felt very angry and said to myself, 'I will get it back.' At that very moment I saw it being driven by the thieves. After a chase in which the police were involved, the thieves abandoned the car and ran. I was able to collect my car from a part of South East London.

On the second occasion the police had found my car abandoned in the middle of the road in the very same area, before I had even realized it had been stolen. As I stood there looking at the car I noticed a little rust in the nearside wing and also that the bonnet had a few scratch marks on it. The driving side door also showed signs of wear. I thought, 'As soon as the coming winter is over, I shall have these affected parts renewed.' The next day I had cause to go to the very area where my car had been found, both times it had been stolen. The weather had turned atrocious and it was pouring with rain. I was driving carefully through this area when to my horror I saw another car heading towards me in my lane. I quickly turned the wheel towards the kerb and was hit full on into the driving side of the car. The wing, door and bonnet were completely destroyed. Once again I was to be accused of something of which I was innocent. The other party swore that it was I, and not he, who had lost control and caused the accident. In the early spring of 1985 I did in fact have the very parts I had decided to have renewed, and later on this summer I have to attend a court case concerning this accident that I am positive I shall win.

Various kinds of events were still continuing to take place very frequently in my life, and it was about this time that I once again experienced the movement of yet another object in my home.

Since the day I brought home from the coast John's small case containing many of his small personal belongings I had not looked inside it. It remained in a cupboard unopened. Since I had packed these items in the case to bring home, I was aware of what it contained. After a very long wet spell when I had nothing to do, I decided to get the case out and go through the contents. The very first thing I took from it was a small pocket-sized book on antiques. In this book were very small pictures of figurines that were quite valuable. I wondered if the figurine that John had given me several years prior to his death was among them. Because they were so small I took my magnifying glass from the drawer and studied every detail of each of the small figurines in the book, at the same time picturing in my mind the one the John had given to me and which I kept in my front room behind a glass-fronted part of my large wall unit. Being aware that this figurine was Crown Derby I took it from its place as little as possible for fear of an accident. This was why I tried to visualize the item rather than bring it into the room I was in at the time. I was deeply engrossed in my actions when I thought I heard something or someone in my hallway. I really don't know what I thought I had heard, but was fully aware that no one other than myself could possibly be in the house. I left the room and looked into the hall and then returned to what I was doing without giving another thought to the matter. Whatever had prompted me to look into the hall gave me no cause for alarm, so I continued to look for the figurine. I spend the daytime in my breakfast room and go into the front room during the evening, as I did on this particular evening, and because of my actions earlier decided to take a good look at the figurine to see if I had recalled it correctly. The statue was where it had always stood, on a glass shelf behind the glass door, but now it was turned completely round and the boy was facing the wall. To protect this statue it had been secured on to a square velvet base and the only way it could have been turned into the position it now stood in would have been by removing it from its place, turning the whole base around and then replacing it. So here again was an object that had moved connected with a person who had died.

During this same period of time I desperately needed another car and had spoken about this to a friend on the telephone. As I replaced the receiver my door bell rang. It was a young fellow I knew. Now, although he had no knowledge of my recent car accident, he had called on me to ask if I wanted to buy the car he had for sale. Having looked it over I said no as it was in a very bad condition. He then asked if I would lend him £10 to place the car in the car auctions. I lent him the money and a little later decided to go on an errand along the road although it was pouring with rain. I had only gone a short distance when I spotted a car for sale. I made a note of the phone number to ring and when I returned home I did this and purchased the car. It was not really a very practical car for me and my mechanic agreed, and said it was because it had twin carburettors it was not really suitable, so I decided to get rid of it and obtain a different model. The next day when walking in the same road where I had purchased this car (this is the same road that all my events have taken place in) I met a neighbour whom I only vaguely knew. We walked along together and he suddenly stopped to get into his car. I said, 'I like that,' and jokingly added, 'I'll swap you for my one.' The following day he called me over and showed me how he had cleaned his car up ready for the swap, and showed me all over it, and I thought, 'My God, he has taken me seriously.' Not to go back on my suggestion, I went ahead and we exchanged cars on the 25th of that month.

Now, over the years of owning the car John had given me, John never really understood that the car was very special to me and on several occasions he had suggested that I buy another and allow our daughter to have my car, or he would say how a small estate car would be more practical for me. I agreed, but each time I would say to him, 'No one is ever going to have this car, and even if I buy another I shall put this one in the garage and keep it in good condition.' I now had the small estate car that John had so often advised me to get. My own car is in the garage where it had remained since the repair work was carried out. It is polished and clean and will stay there until 1990 when it will be twenty years old. I have the little estate car to run around in.

Yet another statement made many years ago had come true, but only after a bad event having first taken place as I have realized so often happens, and the events leading to the accident were connected with other desires, once again, like John's heart attack. Many events were to take place before a desire expressed long ago was to materialize and each event was connected in some way. I sometimes felt that I was somehow looking down on all these many events and seeing them taking place all at one time, and the years that separated each event did not exist. I can only describe this feeling by comparing it with watching a film, and how that film may take you back in time over many years to enable the director to tell the story, and yet in 'real' time only a matter of hours expire while you view the whole story. Such is my memory that each and every one of the unaccountable events of my life lie in my mind like one continuous story.

Although I own several watches, I have never worn a watch

for many years. As far as I am able to recall it must be some twenty years or so. I refuse to be dominated by time and resent being made aware of time by carrying it around with me. Once again I am unable to put correctly into words my feelings on this subject, and I only recall the fact that I resent being constantly aware of time when I am asked what the time is and reply that 'I don't wear a watch' if asked why not. (I have made the comment about this resentment automatically rather than having thought in any way on the subject.)

In the meantime, my life with all its continuous accusations continued into 1984 until the ninth month. The 25th September 1984 to be precise, and then my whole way of thinking was to change.

9

From 25th September 1984 onwards, I began to become fully awake at around 3 am each morning, just as when I had the compulsive daydream. My mind was filled with entirely alien thoughts, different from any others I had experienced throughout my life. Unlike the daydreams, from which I had drawn no conclusions and which at the time appeared meaningless, from these new compulsive thoughts came the answers to the mystery surrounding my entire life.

During this early period of wakefulness, if there was something I did not quite understand, I would wake up several days running with the same thoughts in my mind but presented in different ways. After a week or so this was no longer happening as I had begun to grasp the full meaning of the thoughts, and a complete new understanding was emerging. The many events in my life were now to act as proof that all I was now discovering was true. Whereas in the past I had concentrated the whole of my mental investigations on myself and my own personal and unusual experiences, the picture now emerging involved not just me but everyone on this earth.

Since my childhood, when I ceased to believe in God, I found, as I matured, that I acquired an open mind on religion. While I was never really convinced there was a God, nor of the truth of the Bible, I never condemned those who did believe. I have always thought that if a person finds contentment by believing in the Bible, then this must be good. (I have never even read the Bible, only heard quotes from it.) Now, however, I feel positive there is indeed someone far greater than us. Not one who guides us through life but one who has given us complete power during our time on earth to control our own lives and destiny and even our own deaths.

Whoever this is plays no part whatsoever during our lifespan.

Having said this, I must make it quite clear I have no idea at all of what takes place before birth or what will take place after death. My findings concern only life here on this planet. Even though I feel positive that I have the KEY, I have no suggestions as to how the planets or the universe are involved, nor what is the relationship with the forces of water and the earth's magnetism – though I do feel certain that all of these play a role in our lives.

During the first stage of my new thoughts I found time and again that I used the 'winners of the horses' episode as a reason to accept what was now being revealed to me. It was as if this period, which kept returning to my mind, was being shown to me as an example, a proof, of what I was learning from an invisible teacher.

I rethought all the events of this time and in my mind I asked myself the following questions:

If I had not felt desperate for money and determined to dream the winners would it have happened?

Was it not because of past events that I believed I could dream the winners?

Was it not prior to sleep that I ordered myself to dream?

Was it not on awakening that I knew which horses to bet on?

Was this not all a combination of emotions, belief and a command?

With the answers to these questions, I understood.

I had commanded my subconscious mind – and it had obeyed.

This was the beginning of all that was to be revealed to me about the subconscious mind. I discovered that as we lead our lives and communicate with our families, relations, friends and many other people, so, in an entirely different dimension the subconscious mind of every one of us is doing exactly the same. There is another life within us, going on at the same time as our ordinary life. Nature intended these two lives to be lived on different levels and although they are connected we were and are supposed to be unaware in our thinking mind of the other mind and its life.

Since nothing is perfect, people like me and others with so-called 'gifts' are accidentally penetrating the subconscious world at various points. While in everyday life we have many outward ways to communicate, such as speaking, writing, using the telephone or radio, so the subconscious mind has its own perfectly complete communications system including its own kind of transmitter and receiver.

It does not need, as we do, a body to carry out its purpose in life. It has the ability to go back in time or even years ahead, laying out the destiny of its master, the Thinking Mind.

The subconscious can be likened to the 'Genie of the Lamp' and must throughout life obey every command made by its master and its master alone.

Since time and distance mean nothing in the world of the subconscious we sometimes remember what we are meant to forget on awakening from sleep. We may then relate our thoughts. When, at a later date, the event we spoke of takes place, it is held we have a talent for predicting the future, especially if it happens to us on several occasions.

I understand also now that no command can be obeyed unless an emotion of some kind is involved. The order put to the subconscious mind must be supported by a wish, a desire and either love, hatred, determination, greed, hostility, sincerity or even a positive 'I am going to'. Each kind of emotion will set in motion a chain of very ordinary events via the subconscious mind which will lead to the command being obeyed – sooner or later.

Not one meeting or conversation in life is by chance. Everything is part of one of the many chains of events laid out by the subconscious mind in the process of obeying orders.

If you can, imagine a huge mountain containing millions of pieces of jigsaw puzzles, some pieces fitting many more than just one puzzle, thus making the whole procedure of completing them all the more difficult. Then, to make it even more complicated, each puzzle as it is completed must also interlock with the puzzle emerging from many other people's own mountains of pieces. Now can you grasp the magnitude of what is happening? Even as some puzzles are made whole, so more and more pieces are falling on top of the pile. Some puzzles which are waiting to be completed have lain on the heap for many years before they are finished. Eventually the puzzles are being completed and fewer and fewer pieces are being added. So the mountain gets smaller and smaller until at last only one puzzle has yet to be completed. The final one.

Throughout life this is how the commands of the subconscious mind occur. We *ourselves* decide and the subconscious obeys, until that final puzzle, which we ourselves laid out, is completed. We then die.

Since time does not exist in the world of the subconscious, the duration of even a very long life here on earth, compared to that of someone who lives for a very short time, is of little difference compared to eternity, where the spirit of the subconscious mind will return once death on earth takes place.

In the event of a major disaster, many final puzzles may be completed in the interlocking of pieces, with each person concerned fated to meet for that one occasion via the millions of impulses sent out by the subconscious mind prior to the tragedy taking place.

Even whilst the final puzzle is in the process of being completed we are each aware that our days are numbered and may well carry out certain actions that will cause someone to say after our death: 'It's as if he knew.'

Throughout our day our subconscious mind is ahead of time as we know it, just as we are aware of what will happen in a film we are watching for a second time. It sometimes happens that the thinking mind accidentally enters into the subconscious world for as second or two. So, on arriving at a strange destination we can be alarmed to realize that we have seen the place before, although we know full well this is the first visit and we should know nothing about it.

Throughout our waking hours we are actually transmitting thoughts to, and receiving thoughts from, each person we think about, for whatever reason.

Throughout life, the world of the subconscious mind is transmitting and receiving very strong thoughts from our immediate family and close friends.

Nothing that happens in life is a coincidence. If you think of a tune before someone hums it or it is sung on the radio, your subconscious mind has caused your awareness by moving

106

ahead of our time.

A new-born baby, whose subconscious mind is yet undeveloped as it has not learned to desire things from life and is not 'aware', receives transmitted thoughts from members of the family. These play a role in forming the child's character. As the child matures, it too transmits to the family circle. Distance makes no difference: you may decide to write to a relative living thousands of miles away and you yourself receive a letter written at the same time – again, the result of the transference of thought.

Identical twins are usually very much more in tune with each other as they were born of the same conception. Even if parted at birth and unaware of each other's existence, their subconscious minds never lose contact. If they discover each other after many years they usually learn that they have led almost identical lives, relative to their circumstances. They receive identical impulses.

A mother suddenly becomes aware that something has happened to her child, perhaps an accident leading to death. What she experiences is not a premonition but a sudden knowledge or feeling caused by the cessation of the thoughts transmitted to her since birth by her child. It has suddenly been cut off – 'Something has gone out of her life', quite literally.

How many times have you thought of a person only suddenly to meet them? Or spoken of someone and they call on you? The subconscious minds involved 'linked' up before you physically met.

I believe that good or evil, throughout life, are man-made and not, as I thought as a child, derived from God. It is only Man who claims God is responsible for the good. I now believe that just as Man has been given all that is required to determine his own life on Earth, he has also been given guide books to enable him to use what he has with wisdom to find contentment and happiness while on Earth. He has been given the Bible and other holy books in many different cultures.

As I have stated, since the subconscious must obey every command, good or bad, our whole life is based purely on our thinking. Should we feel and think anger or harm to another in a positive way and carry out the act we can be punished by law. But also at sometime in our life we will ourselves receive similar treatment to that which we desired for someone else. Although the subconscious mind serves only its master and assisted by contacting the victim, the puzzle could not be said to be completed until the master was likewise served. On the other hand the victim would have experienced fear, fear generated by a 'certain knowledge'. This was fear that something bad was going to happen and the thoughts then transmitted made him the victim.

Fear is one of the strongest emotions and works overtime throughout the world, causing much sorrow and grief.

Love, too, works the same way, and again such thoughts and acts involving kindness eventually 'return to the starter', This process underlies the Bible saying 'As ye sow, so shall ye reap.'

Many times during my life when studying people I have noted many occasions when a person has been very pleased about something bad happening to someone he disliked. Then, usually a year or so later, a very similar thing has afflicted that person himself. On the more pleasant side, when somebody has expressed pleasure at something good happening to another, I have observed that the well-wisher too has had 'good luck'. This has happened more times than I could ever put down to coincidence, and formed a part of my original thinking. Now I understand how these things came to pass.

I liken my new thoughts to the achievements of a man who has been given every kind of tool needed to accomplish a task, and then left to get on with it – only answering to the provider of the tools when the work was completed. So, have we not been given all the tools? Maybe the Bible and other holy books do not contradict themselves as is often claimed, but merely explain in different ways a fundamental teaching.

Do not religious texts consist of many stories, just as my dreams and compulsive thoughts came in varying forms when providing me with a message?

Within my mind I now viewed the entire picture, and how easy it was to understand my life and its many mysteries. Each event was no longer mysterious at all now that my emotional demand for the truth had been granted, in the very same ways that all that I desired throughout my life had also been granted. I understood as well why this had not materialized before during my long search. I had never, truly understood that the common denominator in all my strange events was in fact the vital part that my emotions played in all that had taken place, until now.

In late February, because of all the stress in my life, for the first time ever, I demanded of my subconscious mind to know exactly what was taking place, and this was a direct, clear and emotional order. To obtain this knowledge I had accidentally used the same procedure, as I had been doing unknowingly throughout my life, of using the power of the subconscious mind. And the subconscious mind had to obey. Yet again, as was usual with all my events, it obeyed on the ninth month. The other thing I noted was the fact that I was born on 25th November, so I must have been conceived in the latter part of February. It was in the latter part of February 1984 that I conceived the idea of demanding the truth. Although it is not practical to include them in this book, there are very many other observations that I made throughout the years which should at a later date be included in further research into my findings.

How relieved I was to discover I was not the kind of freak I had imagined myself to be, but was only different in that I had been born with an unintended insight and contact with the world of the collective subconscious. Over the years, while aware that something was not as it should be, through my constant mental search for the truth, I had developed even greater involvement with this inner world. I realized too how conceited I had been, always assuming that when an unusual event occurred, it was entirely my doing. Now I can see that each person involved was also enacting a part of a chain of events of their own making and what transpired was as imperative for each of them as for me.

I have long maintained that water appears to play an important part in a range of phenomena and I could now understand the basic ingredients of the life we lead.

Water, electricity, personal or mental magnetism, emotion and *belief*, together with our outer world and the superior world of the subconscious.

Once I had received a full understanding I was also to receive compulsive instructions that now dominated my mind in the same way that other compulsive thoughts had done throughout my life. My first compulsion was to contact the married couple whom I had last contacted in 1981, after completing my compulsive writings, and had not seen since. At this time it was so near to the Christmas holiday that I felt I should wait until the New Year before contacting them. But inside I felt an urgency and knew that it had to be before Christmas 1984 and not in the New Year. Even today I do not understand why this had to be so. I got in touch with them and they graciously agreed to meet and discuss my findings. This meeting took place just a matter of days before Christmas 1984. The writing of my findings are a result of that meeting.

Once again a compulsive daydream was becoming a reality. The daydream I spoke of at the beginning of chapter eight. It was after so many false accusations by members of my family and then outsiders that I was led to demand the answers. There was a married couple whom I was prepared to talk to. It was always Christmas-time in my daydream. I was aware that I knew quite a lot about life, but did not wish to speak of my knowledge. (Only a very few people are aware of this manuscript. None of my friends or relatives have any knowledge whatsoever.) And, throughout this book, I just cannot find it in myself to disclose my identity.

So now I wondered why was I fourteen in the daydream? Why was it America? And why 1984?

Now that I had a deeper understanding about the events of my life, the explanations were both simple and clear, and to show this I will go back over these events, but this time with a very clear understanding of how each of them took place. This way I will at the same time be explaining all that I had learnt from my invisible teacher. The only way I could comprehend my new thoughts was by using the many unnatural events that had taken place in my life as clues that had been given in advance and would now fit the whole puzzle together. Just like a detective solving a murder, who collects all the clues and then the whole picture of what took place reveals itself, whereas each clue on an individual basis meant nothing at all. It was my collective events that revealed the existence of the collective subconscious and another existence. Life within a life.

Now I was aware of the existence of the subconscious world I realized that during my research into the many strange and seemingly unaccountable events, I had looked on each one, quite mistakenly, as individual occurrences. Now, however, for the first time I was able to bring all that had happened throughout my life together as though the years between the various events did not exist. All my 'events' now presented themselves in my mind in several chains of circumstances, and yet each chain connected at various points to another. These chains were divided from the very important decisions that were to be taken in my life. When I reflected on the average semi-important events, and the very minor everyday actions concerning small talk with various friends and relations, on telephone calls I may have received or made during the course of the day, I could now see so clearly that a mixture of events taken from the minor chain had on each occasion repeated itself when an event from the important chain was to materialize. Then because I knew it would be impossible to write in words all that I could so clearly see and understand within my mind, there came the instructions to write them down in thought chains. These were to consist of the events that had occurred after my commands to the subconscious had taken place. This way I was able to see the entire picture, and could take events from over a long span of my life and bring them together by this method. To draw a simple analogy, if we were to hold a conversation with someone and said only a part of it, then allowed several years to pass before holding the next part of the conversation and so on until over the course of many years we finally told the whole story, each part of the conversation at the time of being told would have made very little sense and would quite naturally cause concern because we had not understood what it was about. But, if at the end of the period of time we joined together all that had been said throughout those years, we would then for the first time understand. It was in the very same way that I had been presented bit by bit over many years with various aspects of the subconscious world, and now for the first time the entire picture was brought together and it became so obvious how each strange event had in fact occurred, and also how each was a continuation of the sameness evolving from the chains that were to connect and link up at various stages.

In the next chapter I will show how these chains were taking place in my life, and will include some of the events I have described in previous chapters, leaving out many other details and events that still remain in my mind since too much has taken place to include everything in this manuscript. It is the very fact that I am aware of so much, and you the reader are aware of so little that you are at an unfair disadvantage when accepting my findings. Nevertheless, I sincerely hope that I will supply sufficient evidence to prove the existence of the world within.

Because I have been unable to include here every strange event that has taken place in my life, or even give a very full account of the lesser details which must be included, I have been unable to show a clear picture of the various chains I speak of. However, I will attempt to do so now.

The important chains concern birth, marriage, our children, death, family members, the many important decisions that could alter the course of our lives, such as purchasing property, leaving one's country, and even the upheaval of returning from another country, our beliefs, and so on.

The less important chains concern what type of car would be best to buy; deciding what we could or could not afford to buy; what to do with a property once purchased; what furniture would suit our home; the best way to invest our savings; where to go on holiday; the school we should send our children to; how to raise our children, and many other non crucial decisions.

The very minor chains consist of: what to have for dinner; where to go for an evening out; whether we should pay a visit to such and such a friend, and all the various actions and commitments one may do or be obliged to do in the course of a normal day. Even idle chatter and conversation are part of these chains.

But apart from there being these three groups of chains, concealed within each group there are individual chains in operation that from time to time connect. One from the lesser group may become involved with a chain from the important group. But those from the minor group are involved with every chain from every group, as I hope to show in the following pages. This fact, therefore, makes the minor chains very significant to my findings. It must also be remembered that the main part of our lives revolve around what we do, who we meet, what we hear and what we say each day of our lives, whereas events concerning the higher chains are present in the background until they have to be dealt with.

In my life I have discovered that with every important event that has taken place since the day I moved into the second house after leaving the East End of London, 11, 14 and 25 are involved, and the fact that $11 + 14 = 25$ must also be taken into consideration. I was born on the 25th of the 11th month. The dominant number in my life however is number nine. This number is of great significance. We moved house on my ninth birthday. The number of the house was 81. $8 + 1 = 9$. $9 \times 9 = 81$.

I met John in June and we married in February, two months which have also featured in many events that have taken place.

Numbers and dates must really be considered to belong in a minor category. No one is shocked or surprised if you say 'It's my birthday today' or 'I lived at such and such a number house', because they are very isolated insignificant details about life. But to gather all the many dates that are important in your life together and discover that during your lifetime everything revolved around just four numbers then this must be of great importance. It was these dates that connected many of the chains along with many other minor details that repeated themselves at random when various strange events took place. Many, many were connected with just one particular road.

Among the few events of my life I have included in this book many small details recur. For example, on four occasions it was after a special journey to the shops that a desire was granted. It was because I had to make a special trip to the shops that I met the owner of the vision house which we purchased. It was because John, who normally purchased his own materials for work, asked me to go to the only shop that sold the special paint he required that I passed and entered the estate agent, which resulted in our buying a piece of property. It was because I wished John to meet a man in a shop that we were destined to meet Mr Evans for a second time. We viewed his house, which was in keeping with the property chain, and yet Mr Evans belonged in my personal

113

search for the truth concerning my strange way of life. He connected these two chains, but then faded from the scene when he failed to sell his house to John. (He also provided the two gold ashtrays that I had predicted to Kay and Ted.) Three events I have mentioned have been connected with cleaning my car: the first time, when approached by the home help to assist her with the elderly man who had suffered a heart attack; the second when the attempted suicide took place; and the third when I decided to renew parts in the spring, the day before the car crash.

I was visiting my mother the day I felt an urgent impulse to return home and found my house on fire. I was also visiting my mother the day I felt I had to return home and prevented the suicide. On two occasions, (the day John died, and the day Kevin died), I had cause to speak to a policeman about a car outside my home, and on both occasions the policeman was walking along the same part of the same road.

I very seldom dream, yet I had two extremely vivid dreams. One concerned Bill, my brother-in-law and the other a young friend called Kevin. John appeared in both dreams, and although these two dreams took place a few months apart, Bill's and Kevin's funerals took place on the same day. Each time I won funeral expenses back, one week after the funeral had taken place.

Too many times throughout my search I have been aware of these minor details and could not dismiss them as being of no importance.

If the police were to see the same man in the crowd after many fires had been started there would be no way that they could ignore the fact that he had something to do with the fires. This is how I felt about these small details.

Names, too, repeated themselves over the years. Evans, Wallis and Sturd were links in the chain of events arising from the book, then the chain connected to the property chain when I discovered that the first lease taken out on my vision house was by a Mrs Sturd. (And as I have mentioned about the number 9 it was taken out on 9.9.1909.)

It was a Mr Tiller who introduced John to factory maintenance. Years later I discovered I was working for his brother in the north of England, also Mr Tiller. My mother's maiden name was Tiller. Her married name was Daly. John's mother's christian name was Olive. The woman who purchased the small flat John lived in at the coast was a Mrs Olive Daly.

10

THOUGHT CHAIN OF
EVENTS QUOTED IN CHAPTER FOUR

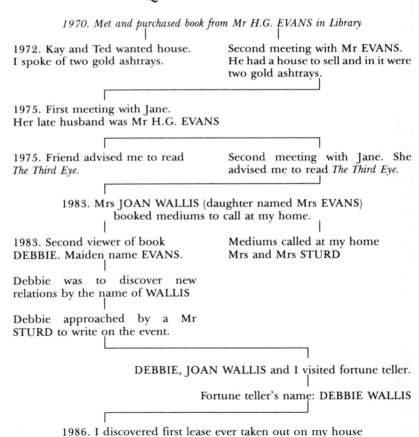

1970. Met and purchased book from Mr H.G. EVANS in Library

1972. Kay and Ted wanted house.
I spoke of two gold ashtrays.

Second meeting with Mr EVANS.
He had a house to sell and in it were
two gold ashtrays.

1975. First meeting with Jane.
Her late husband was Mr H.G. EVANS

1975. Friend advised me to read
The Third Eye.

Second meeting with Jane. She
advised me to read *The Third Eye*.

1983. Mrs JOAN WALLIS (daughter named Mrs EVANS)
booked mediums to call at my home.

1983. Second viewer of book
DEBBIE. Maiden name EVANS.

Mediums called at my home
Mrs and Mrs STURD

Debbie was to discover new
relations by the name of WALLIS

Debbie approached by a Mr
STURD to write on the event.

DEBBIE, JOAN WALLIS and I visited fortune teller.

Fortune teller's name: DEBBIE WALLIS

1986. I discovered first lease ever taken out on my house
was to a Mrs STURD in 1909.

This is just one example of several chains that had taken place in my life that I could now see in my mind. Even meeting Mrs Joan Wallis was through yet another event. I met her for the first time in my club, we became friendly and she mentioned how all that Sunday afternoon she and her husband had been trying to locate the owner of a flat that was for sale. I asked where the flat was, and discovered I was the owner of the flat, which I had very recently placed on the market after John's death. (The flat was part of the house we purchased after my impulse to go into the estate agents as I described in a previous chapter.) So can you begin to get the picture of how I would have to go back over many events, and branch off in many directions covering many other events, to find where this chain really began?

Because Debbie, Joan and I had become associated with each other, yet another chain was going on at one and the same time, but this time mainly involving everyday events and of a very minor nature. I had been given a large black plastic bucket which I decided to keep in my garage for making up size when decorating. Then I mistakenly thought my deep freezer had gone wrong and a little later discovered that it was in fact a second deep freezer that had water running from underneath. I was very annoyed as this freezer, although out of guarantee, was the newer one of the two, and I was told that it could not be repaired. The seal had gone. Knowing that the booking to visit the fortune teller had been made, I set out to the shops and ordered a new Indesit deep freezer. Having crossed the road of the main shopping centre, I met Debbie. On her arm she had a new black bucket identical to the one I had so recently been given. I told her how I had just purchased a new deep freezer, to which she said, 'You should have come into the shop where I work and I would have got you a discount.' I asked where she worked and she pointed out a shop just a little away from where I had made my purchase. It was a discount store of electrical appliances. I then informed her that we had made the booking and made arrangements where we should all meet, but added, 'Anyway I shall see you at the club this evening.' That evening I called on Joan as was usual to go to the club, but she told me that she could not afford to go, and went on to explain how her deep freezer had gone wrong and she had just had a new Indesit

117

deep freezer delivered. Almost every occasion that Joan and I go to the club together it transpires that we have either cooked the same meals that day or had on impulse decided to do the very same thing. Joan, by the way, lives in the very road where so much of the unusual has taken place in my life. I had never seen her before our meeting at the club since the road is a fairly long one and I am invariably in my car anyway.

Back in October or November 1985 I was in the process of redecorating a room and was ready to paste and apply the wallpaper the morning after one of my evenings out to my club. On the way home that evening I thought it would be a good idea if I were to make up the size when I got home, in readiness for the following morning. Once home, however, I did not relish the thought of going to the end of the garden in the dark to get the black bucket. I then had to post an urgent letter, and walked along the road to do so, once again the road of my events. I had gone about a third of the length of the road when I noticed a black object lying on the pavement. It was a black bucket, identical to the one in my garage. I took it home and made up the size. I now have two black buckets!

On yet another occasion recently I told a young relative of mine not to stand on the small plastic cup as she was doing, or she would break it. I then added that the cup was very similar to the kind of cup children used to use in the olden days to roll dice from when playing Snakes and Ladders. I then left the house and drove along the road to pick up Joan for our usual visit to the club. As Joan stepped out of the car she stooped and picked something up from the ground. I asked what she had found and she opened her hand and showed me the blue dice she had picked up. Then I also spotted a red one lying on the ground. She gave me the blue one and I dropped the two of them into my coat pocket. Later that evening having given them to my young relative she sat at the table rolling them from the cup I had previously chided her for trying to break.

Before 1984 when events of this kind were so obviously taking place in my life they caused me much concern. Now, however, I fully understood that all that was taking place was the result of the transference of thoughts that take place once we connect ourselves to each other. Obviously Debbie, Joan and I were to have each other on our minds since we were planning on meeting and we were merely transmitting our actions back and forth. The very fact that both Joan and I were to require a new deep freezer can only suggest that because Joan had transmitted to me that she needed to purchase a new one, I then received an impulse to believe that my deep freezer had gone wrong also, and because of this mistaken belief I had actually caused the second deep freezer to break down, just as I explained earlier how our thoughts effect electrical equipment. Remember too that Debbie was at that time working in a shop that contained several deep freezers and even this fact was in some way connected. Because Joan had her new deep freezer delivered before I had selected mine, she then had transmitted to me the make of her new freezer and although I had several makes to choose from, via impulses from Joan, I selected the very same make as she.

While all I am trying to convey in this book is so clear in my mind, the ability to write it is very difficult indeed, but I do hope I have demonstrated yet another chain of events, (thus proving how thoughts and actions are being transmitted) along an unending chain. Via Debbie and other friends and associations of people, and Joan also, this chain affecting our lives was at the same time branching off in many directions like an electrical current passing through many outlets that have various equipment attached for many different purposes. So too do these electrical impulses pass through human beings resulting in every aspect of life that man has created on this earth, whether it be for good or bad.

Mob violence originates in just one person's mind via an emotional command to his subconscious. Maybe a man has been rightly or wrongly sacked, and this causes him to feel angry and bitter and to have a deep desire for revenge. He relates his feelings and anger to his workmates who in turn think about him and his dismissal. They then receive his transmitted thoughts of revenge. They too transmit to their friends and so on until the anger has been transmitted to an ever-expanding circle of people, and mob violence takes place. Yet among these violent people many are decent law-abiding citizens caught up in these transmitted desires to destroy. Many of them would probably have sacked the man concerned themselves had he been employed by them. This merely shows how we and our emotional thoughts can create events on a very large scale. We condemn the world we live in yet we created it, and nothing will alter until the truth I am trying to reveal is fully understood.

Because I know that results of my desires are all in some way or other connected to those around me, there is no way that I could ever imagine that I am special or that my life is any different from other people's. I do, however, accept the fact that I am different inasmuch as I have been vaguely aware of what was taking place. And it was merely this awareness that caused me to think I was different. Although I have pointed out just two chains of events that were taking place in my life, there are others that I could very easily quote that were going on at the same time. The fact that I decided on impulse to make the size just before finding the bucket, and the impulse I received to tell the young relative about how we rolled dice as children, was evidence that my subconscious mind, being ahead of time as we know it, was aware that these items were to be found, and almost as though I had already found them I was caused to think and speak as I did. I accidentally became aware of my subconscious knowledge of these future events. Nature did not intend us to have this awareness, so the fact that I did have it accounted for much of the mystery that has dominated my life since childhood. I too at this time am aware that I become aware of attitudes of people's private feelings without words being spoken. And throughout my life have been reacting to this knowledge. Either by trusting them or not wishing to associate with them. Always at a later date remarks would confirm this knowledge.

I would now like to relate more recent incidents that have occurred in my life, that may easily be proven as having taken place, although each person who played a part is completely unaware of the entire story.

In May 1985, after an extremely exhausting day, I fell asleep as soon as my head hit the pillow and the dream that I had that night was as clear in every detail as a show on television would be. I dreamt that I was driving my car towards our local hospital and beside me sat a relative with whom I seldom had any contact. He sat beside me staring at the road ahead. Although he had not spoken a word I knew I was taking him to hospital because he was very worried about bad pains in his chest. I said, 'Bill, there is no need to worry, John had chest pains and he is all right.' (John being my late husband.) The scene suddenly changed and I was now in the process of moving into a ground floor flat. There were large packing cases everywhere but I could see no furniture. I entered the lounge where there were more packing cases and found John by the fireplace with plaster made up to carry out some work on it. I said to him, 'Leave that now and let's get unpacked.' I then left the room to search for the cooker to prepare something for John to eat. When I returned to the lounge John was now seated at a large packing case eating a Chinese Take-Away, something neither John nor I had ever eaten. I then awoke and immediately became aware that this was no ordinary dream and decided that I had to speak of it to someone before and not after the meaning of it transpired.

As was usual on a Monday afternoon a sister of mine paid me a visit and I decided to relate my dream from the previous night to her. She was in contact with the relative who had been in my dream, and after I had told her the dream, she said that Brenda, another sister of ours, was going to visit the family of whom I had dreamt that very evening. Two days later, on the Wednesday, she called again and informed me that Brenda had paid the intended visit and while there had been told that Bill was very worried about pains in his chest and was going to the hospital to find out the cause. It also transpired that a Chinese man had wanted to purchase the shop they owned for a Chinese-Take-Away but had withdrawn after the budget which put VAT on hot take-away foods. They now had a buyer who wanted the premises for a warehouse to store stock in. Bill and his wife had been out and put a deposit on a ground floor flat, and Bill's wife asked Brenda to ask Margie (the sister I told the dream to) if her husband would disconnect her cooker when they were ready to move. After Bill had had tests at the hospital, my sister (his wife) was informed that he had only a matter of months to live.

The sale of the shop went through and they moved into their new flat. That October I had been working very hard all morning, lifting rocks out of a rockery in my garden and shifting a mountain of earth and then relaying the whole area with a newly laid-out rockery. At 2 pm I was absolutely exhausted and went into the house, where I almost immediately fell into a deep sleep in the chair where I was sitting. In the dream that followed I had awakened from this sleep and was amazed to find that although I was in the same chair I was in a room at the front of my house instead of the back. I was positive that I was now awake because I recalled sitting in this very chair after having worked in the garden. Then to my horror John entered the room and although he did not utter a word, I knew he was very angry about something. I also knew it was because I had sold our property and recalled all that I had done since his death. I thought 'No, you are dead,' then because I was so sure that I was awake a terrible thought struck me – I had only dreamt that John had died and because of a dream I had sold our assets. I felt panic rising inside and when he stormed off out of the room I knew he was going to his solicitor, and I started screaming, 'No, no, no, no.' I then awoke for find it was 4 pm and I had slept for two hours. I sat dazed, wondering if I was really awake or was still asleep dreaming.

Once again I related this dream to my sister. That evening I had cause to walk along the road which all my events seem to revolve around and for the first time since I saw a policeman in this road the day John died, I now saw a policeman in almost the very same part of the road, and once again I had cause to approach him regarding a stolen car that had been discarded outside my house some months previously. Having mentioned the car to him I wished I had not done so, recalling the incident of three years before. The next day whilst out in my car I felt a very strong compulsion to park my car and go into a large store knowing full well I had no need to purchase anything. I did as the impulse instructed and on entering the store met a friend who informed me that the previous day a young friend of mine had died. Just a lad of twenty. Friends of his had hoped to see me the day he died but at that time I was working on the rockery. I decided to call on the lad's parents to offer my condolences and to assist in any way I could and also to find out when the funeral was to take place. On the way I met with a friend of the dead lad and inquired from him when the funeral would take place. But he looked puzzled and asked, 'What funeral?'

I said, 'Kevin's funeral.'

He said, 'No, Kevin isn't dead, he's around somewhere,' in a panic stricken voice. I assured him that Kevin was dead and said how sorry I was as I did not know he had been unaware.

He then said almost uncontrollably, 'NO, no, no, no,' just as I had done in my dream.

After the death of John, John's doctor had given me a repeat prescription for Valium tablets to see me through that period. Just a week prior to Kevin's death I found that prescription when clearing out a drawer. Now Kevin's father wanted it, as his own doctor had refused his daughter such a prescription. I agreed with Kevin's father that I would take some of his son's friends in my car to the funeral and I returned home. I then received a phone call from my sister (Bill's wife) to inform me that at six pm the day before, 8th October 1985, Bill had passed away and was to be cremated on 14th October. The very same day that Kevin was to be buried. I attended Kevin's funeral on the morning of 14th October, and the cremation of Bill in the afternoon.

About three months after Bill had died I was for the first time to visit my sister in her new flat. It was identical to the one in my dream. The last time I saw Kevin alive was when he came to me on the date of John's birthday, 26th August, which was a bank holiday and a lovely day. Had all this transpired prior to my findings having been revealed to me, it would all have appeared to be yet many more of the strange happenings I had spent so long researching into and going over and over in my mind as to what they were all about. However, because I now knew the answers all was so clear in my mind, and I will now explain simply by using this new awareness.

Bill, unable to sleep because of the chest pains, would quite naturally think of John, the only member of the whole family to have suffered chest pains prior to his death. It would also be natural that Bill's thoughts would then stray to me, being John's widow. Once he had done this although I was sleeping at the time he merely transmitted all his intentions, concerns and information relating to his life to my subconscious mind, which then presented all this information to me in the form of a dream, proving that the subconscious mind has not only the ability to receive from another but can also relate a story containing in a very clear way all the details.

On each occasion when these dreams took place I was in a

state of exhaustion at the time of dreaming, just as I had been when daydreaming and my thoughts were to come from John's lips. Because John and I on so many occasions worked until we were exhausted I now understand that I must have experienced other meaningful dreams while in this state also, which I ignored, because throughout my long research I had never taken our emotions into consideration.

While sleeping in the same state of exhaustion, Kevin's friends were wanting to tell me of Kevin's death and had also transmitted this information to my subconscious mind. And because the subconscious mind is ahead of time as we experience it, it included into the dream story it was presenting to me, the details of Kevin's friends' reactions on hearing of Kevin's death. It also connected John because it was in fact on John's birthday that I last saw Kevin and they were now both dead.

As I have already stated, when major events take place they link up at intervals with the smaller chains of life. For example, the policeman I met in the same place as the previous policeman had been when John died, and the fact that on each occasion I had cause to speak of a car to him, this not being a habit of mine. Had I wished to mention the car to the police I could quite easily have done so during the months it had stood outside my house. All is taking place via the impulses that are flitting from one to another throughout life. The policeman on impulse had decided to walk that very road, I had an impulse that caused me to have reason to meet him, and so on.

Nothing we do or say is purely voluntary. All result from impulses via the subconscious mind, including the impulse I had received a week prior to requiring the old prescription, to clear out the very drawer it was in, because the subconscious mind was aware that it was soon to be needed. And this prescription too was to be a minor incident that was to link up John's and Kevin's deaths. Once again it was on the 9th of the month that I was informed of the sad news of Bill's death. And the 14th of a month being one of the other dates that play an important role in my life, this happened to be the date of Bill's and Kevin's funerals. I was married to John on the 14th, and the other date that dominates my events is the 25th, the date on which I was born. I have ample proof of this, as I have

124

previously stated.

Although the thinking mind and the subconscious mind are two existences going on at the same time, it was clear in my mind that one could not exist without the other. And that both originate from the same source, the brain. Many fictitious stories are written about intelligences of a far superior level than ours, living on a distant planet. These stories even comprehend that they do not have bodies as we have, yet have mysterious powers of communication. Yet such an existence of superior intelligence dwells within us on our very own planet. Has man not always searched for truth in a complex and distant way? I could see now how the many small coincidences that occur in our lives are of utmost importance, yet have never been taken into consideration by educated researchers, although collectively the events are very important indeed.

These are the events that connect all that takes place in our lives together, yet it is done so cleverly that we are not aware of it. Similarly, everything in life when viewed collectively takes on an entirely different meaning than when looked at on an individual basis. Just as we live our lives communicating with each other, so too does the subconscious mind. Once a full understanding of my teachings became clear, I viewed the whole world and what man through his ignorance had created, a vision impossible for me now to put into words. Analysing my compulsive daydreams as to both why and how they had occurred, I saw that these too involved another aspect of the subconscious world. John's thoughts were transferred to my mind, but they actually appeared in the form of a story with hidden meanings. These only became obvious once the truth was revealed, in each case by John himself.

It was now that I understood the message I had not been able to grasp in my earlier dream concerning the market square. We communicate without words. We are receiving without using our ears. My dream of the friend who needed help when the nun appeared, was an indication that subconsciously time does not exist. The dream in which I saw the circumstances of the death of Kay's son was evidence that our dreams are not entirely our own but can result from the transmission of thoughts from other people's minds.

The dream concerning the lecture given by a doctor and the one in which I spoke poetry showed that while asleep our subconscious mind has contact with other subconscious minds and can also relay the contents of those it has been in contact with through our dreams. Because the scene in the hospital was so modern it could only have come from a contemporary subconscious, and was not knowledge transmitted originally from someone in the past or from a previous life. Someone, somewhere may have been listening to that lecture 'in a daydream' or learning the poem to recite at a later date. This information was sent via their subconscious minds to mine and relayed into my dreams.

Many times I would feel a compulsion to return home earlier than intended, only to receive an important phone call, as on the occasion the young woman was attempting suicide, and my knowledge of the phone call that was to inform me of my mother's death. In each case of this nature covering a whole range of the now, so-called mysteries of life, the person seeking out my number to make the phone call was obviously thinking about me, and had merely transmitted their intentions to me in advance of actually making the call. A medium would, and did, explain this kind of incident as evidence of me being in contact with the dead or having received instructions from my guiding spirit from 'the other side'. Just this one aspect of the power of the subconscious mind in one clean sweep dissolved most of the many mysteries I had for years researched into. With each new understanding so, too, were other groups of strange events also to be explained, and the need to dwell on them vanished. All now appeared so very, very simple and how relieved I was no longer to have to relive in my mind the hundreds of now boring details of all that had taken place. It would now be like constantly asking oneself such questions as, 'How did I learn to write?' 'How did I learn to talk?' and so on.

When you feel unduly concerned about somebody and sense that something is wrong and then at a later date discover that very person died at the very same time you were thinking about them, as I did when Billy Short died in my childhood, don't assume you received a message from their spirit. Note the exact time of the thoughts or uneasiness and you will find that it was a minute or seconds *before* the person died. You received a distress signal before death took place and not after, as is often assumed. What is a minute when glancing at the clock compared with the exact moment someone is dying? In the case of Billy Short, before his death he may well have intended calling at our home the following day as he usually did. And he may have decided either to tell me or ask me something, which created the connection that caused me in return to think of him prior to sleep on the very night he was killed. The photographs he gave away two weeks before his death, this and certain actions of John's before he died that were out of keeping at the time, indicated to me that we are subconsciously aware that our death is imminent and via impulses are instructed to act on this knowledge quite unknowingly.

When I had the impulse to ask Kay if Ted had made out his will, I now understand that Kay herself was subconsciously aware of his coming death having received this knowledge by transmitted thoughts from Ted himself. She in return transmitted this to me which resulted in my asking such a question.

The meeting with the man who sold John the property at the coast can now also easily be explained. After John's death (which took place outside this very property) the previous owner told me how he had wondered what I, John's widow, would do with the property. So, during the time I was trying to dispose of it, he had subconsciously made contact with me, I too wishing to know why the property would not sell. The command was put into operation to be obeyed. When I decided to book a holiday on that particular part of the coast and made mental notes of the date and place of the booking, he too via impulses from his subconscious mind and receiving transmitted thoughts of my intentions, did likewise. Once there, we each received impulses that were to cause us to occupy seats next to each other, and this was to result in our each learning from the other the desires we had asked of our subconscious mind. So easy to see and understand, yet so difficult to put into words. I suppose the most important things to remember when trying to understand the abilities of the subconscious mind are that time, as we know it, does not exist, distance is no barrier and that the life within lives way ahead of our present sense of being, just as we are told that the

127

falling star we see actually fell some four years previously. So complex is time that is it almost an impossibility to comprehend the confusion it causes in our minds.

When I began to understand the full importance of my findings back in 1984 I had the strange ability to see every aspect of what I had been taught at one and the same time. I cannot really relate it in words, but this was how it appeared to dominate my mind. I remembers recalling at that time how we are told that a drowning man sees the whole of his life just as he is leaving, or very close to leaving this life, and I likened it to that. In the case of the second house I had placed on the market which resulted in Joan Wallis and I meeting in the club in a very similar way, I had added yet another mystery to my collection, assuming that I alone had created the incident, as I had so mistakenly been assuming throughout my life. Now I know that what happened was an order being obeyed by her subconscious mind and I just happened to be the end result, the owner of the property she had so desperately tried to locate that Sunday. This was yet further evidence that once instructed, the subconscious mind has the power to locate even strangers and set up such meetings in the process of obeying emotional demands. All transmitted trivialities are the build-up, so to speak, of such demands being obeyed in such a casual manner that we are unaware of what is transpiring. Of course 'Birds of a feather, flock together'. This too applies to all other people with common interests in life. I was quite naturally drawn to people who had also had strange experiences, or others such as mediums and the like who claimed to have special powers such as I thought at that time I had also. And now I could see for the first time how wrong I had been, the many times I had stated that 'I WAS NOT LIKE THEM'. I now understand that they indeed *were* like me, and had been born with various forms of insight into the world of the subconscious mind, which was the very same spirit world that they assumed, quite mistakenly to be 'the other side', as they called it. Now I could understand why most mediums in spite of their so-called associations with the spirit world of the departed, are unable to relate details pertaining to what takes place after death, And why all their messages to grieving relatives relate only to our world.

I understood also that all thoughts transmitted to our

subconscious mind, quite unknowingly from our family and friends, live on long after the death of one of these people has taken place. Even someone who passed away fifty years ago cannot completely leave the earth until the very last person they knew also dies, since their transmitted thoughts live on in every person they associated with throughout their lives. It is this knowledge that is abstracted from people's subconscious minds by those with gifts to do so, who consider themselves special.

If we were to trace way back into the past a chain in reverse, taking our four grandparents and their offspring and then their sixteen grandparents and offspring, the chain of relatives spreads ever wider as we go further back. We soon come to realize that we are all related in some way to each other, certainly within immediate racial groups and eventually far back, world wide. So the family of man exists also in the subconscious world.

In our life we lose track of relations, sometimes because they change their name when married or because they are cousins many times removed, and are then considered as only very distantly related. Not so in the world of the subconscious. And it was because of this that I found a deeper understanding of the recurrences of names that were to affect my life, such as those shown in the thought chain at the beginning of this chapter.

I am sure that by now you are beginning, if only vaguely, to understand all that I am trying so desperately to convey in my uneducated way. But remember my findings did not come from my thinking mind, they are not conclusions that I arrived at, they are the result of a positive demand to my subconscious mind to provide the answers, and just as all my desires materialize, so too this desire did also.

I would like to review the times during my life when I became aware of having predicted the future, either by means of a compulsive statement or, as in Canada, when I actually saw the events in my mind so convincingly that it was as though I was thinking of a past event rather than a future one. Because on these occasions I was in fact living temporarily in a country other than my own, it was a natural thing to daydream or even think about a future time when I would once again be making an important change in my life. And because I was thinking in the future my subconscious mind merely gave me in various ways, details of the time I was so concerned with, including an actual vision of the very house we were to eventually purchase. Although each person is also very discreetly supplied with such information, I was aware that this information was a truth about my future, basing this belief on the many other occasions when such happenings had taken place. Because the average person has other priorities of thought, all the intricacies I have been aware of throughout my life simply continue unnoticed. Had I not been aware that something was not quite as it should have been when I was a young child, I too would have had other distractions to occupy my thoughts. Having a remarkable memory to assist in making the connections of my previous thoughts to all that afterwards occurred, was equally significant. So, did I choose to be the way I am? Or was I meant to be the way I am? I have no clear-cut answers to these and many other questions that I ask myself. I have no illusions about myself. I have no special powers, I am just an ordinary person and I now know that I alone am responsible for everything that has happened to me throughout my personal life, good and bad, and that every single person who was able to influence my happiness or sorrow was drawn to me by me, myself in the first place. Those who have avoided my company were pushed away by me. All this was to be so because I wanted to know the answers and I had to be involved throughout my life with people and situations that were eventually to lead me to the frame of mind I was in when I demanded the truth.

So, too, therefore, is everyone else responsible for the lives they lead. We each create our own lives whether in riches, poverty, happiness or misery.

11

I spent a period of time at the home of cousin Ivy before my findings were revealed to me, and she witnessed several of my unaccountable events, which she had become extremely interested in after having read my compulsive writings of 1981. These I had then realized were intended for her benefit and not as I had mistakenly believed at the time of writing them, for the research organization. The estate agent who was to sell the property on my behalf had suggested that I speculate on the lower flat and have central heating installed. However, never having thought this property worth having money spent on it, I discussed this with cousin Ivy. She suggested that I install convector heaters, the same as in the two upper flats. I agreed that this would be more economical. When meeting the estate agent for the first time, he asked which part of London I came from. He then went on to say that he had spent his childhood in the same part of the East End of London that I had moved from when I was a child. He began to say, 'The school I went to was,' when I interrupted him

'Before you tell me the name of the school, was it by any chance a small Roman Catholic school called . . . ?' to which he looked amazed, and said,

'Yes.'

It was the very school I had attended at the age of three.

I began work preparing the flat very early the morning following our agreement to install convector heaters, and worked all day convinced that this was my intention. I made a list of all the materials that would be required the following day, with the intention of shopping for them first thing the next morning. Cousin Ivy called to see me and said, 'You know I have been thinking, why not just buy a nice secondhand electric fire for the lounge and let the purchasers of the property decide what heating they want?'

'Yes, of course,' I replied. 'That is the answer. I'll look at fires tomorrow morning when I go for materials.'

The next morning three of us arrived at the nearby shopping centre very early and since the shops were only just beginning to open, we decided to go into a café first and have breakfast. Across the road from the café I spotted a man in the process of opening his secondhand shop who was carrying items from his estate car into the shop. I walked across the road and enquired if he had a fairly modern secondhand electric fire. He said, 'No I am afraid I don't deal in the more expensive items, but try this phone number.' He took from the dashboard of his car the name and phone number of a man who had come into his shop the previous day wanting to sell him an electric fire. Having phoned the man, it was agreed that we would call on him to look at the fire he had to sell. He gave me his full address and said he would leave his front door open in case he did not hear the doorbell.

Three of us sat drinking our tea and one of us laughingly said, 'What if we walk into the wrong house?'

Having found the road we were seeking, we found the number and sure enough the door was open. We rang the bell several times and got no reply so all three of us stepped into the hall to try to find the owner. I suddenly said, 'I think we are in the wrong house,' and we all quickly ran outside the front door just as the owner appeared. We had mistakenly gone to a Close of the same name (instead of Road), and were in fact in the wrong house. We then proceeded to the correct address and discovered the fire was the very one I required. It fitted perfectly into the space for it with just a one inch gap all round. The man who sold the fire to me explained that it was almost new but having recently moved from London, just a few miles from my home, he had no use for it since he now had central heating in his newly-acquired home.

During yet another conversation with cousin Ivy in the flat I was papering, I suddenly interrupted her to tell her I had become aware that something was wrong with the doctor who attended my husband back in London. She said, 'As soon as you get home and find out what it is, let me know.' I returned to London that weekend and on the Monday decided to pay a visit to the doctor to pay for the prescription of Valium he had given me. (He was John's private doctor.) When I arrived at his surgery I went to enter the waiting room as usual but was told I could not go in because, on the very day I had suspected something was wrong that room, which also contained the cabinet with all the patients' folders, had caught fire, destroying many records, maybe including John's.

Now these events and many more took place prior to my findings being revealed to me, and during one of cousin Ivy's many discussions on what was taking place in my life, she suggested that perhaps I was living ahead of time as we know it. I replied, 'Then how would this account for when I have known the future as much as three years or so ahead, as I did in the case of my vision house?' Since this did not tie all the loose ends together, it was yet another theory to be discarded. Now, however, I believe her assumption to be correct, since I now understand that when I predicted the future well in advance it was, as I have pointed out, at times when I was mentally thinking so deeply of the future. I so often become aware of events a short time before they become reality because I am in fact to a certain degree living my life ahead with my subconscious mind. This is perhaps an inadequate description, but I will continue in the hope that the rest of this chapter will give a clearer understanding of this statement.

After my findings were revealed I did make several experiments with my new-found knowledge and will now relate them.

Because of all the bad feelings that had arisen in 1983 and 1984 concerning close members of my family, I wanted as little as possible to do with them, and they felt the same, since they sincerely believed wrong of me. One night in bed I thought very emotionally about one of these people in particular and said over and over in my mind, naming the person, 'You should feel extremely guilty, you are now feeling very guilty,' until I fell asleep. I awoke very early the following morning which was a Sunday, and even though I had been up several hours it was still only about 7 am when my doorbell rang. Quite forgetting what I had done the previous night, I opened the door and there stood the very relative I had experimented with the previous night, who rarely called on me any more. She explained that she had been unable to sleep

133

all night long and had given up trying at 5 am, and got up from bed, even though she usually had a lie-in on a Sunday. She had called on me as she wanted to know if I needed her help in any way. What further proof did I need of the accuracy of my findings?

One Saturday evening I received a phone call from a very distressed cousin Ivy to tell me that her car had been stolen near her home at the coast. It meant very much to her although it was many years old, because she had owned it since new and it was a very much sought-after model. The police said they doubted if she would ever see it again. She was phoning me in desperation to ask if I could put my findings into operation and get her car back. I then assured her that this would happen within a week and the police would need to fingerprint it before she was to collect it.

Two weeks to the day of that phone call I received a second one from her to inform me that on the Saturday following the theft the police contacted her to say that they had found her car and fingerprinted it, and if she would care to collect it the following day, it was in the East End of London near to where I was born. (She had to drive past the house I now live in to collect the car but did not stop as she knew I would not be at home.) Now, contrary to my old concept of believing all such events were of my making, I now understood that she had made the emotional demand of her subconscious mind and I just happened to be one of the people whom she received an impulse to phone for assistance. The part I played was merely to strengthen the belief that she would get the car back. The policeman who found the car must have received an impulse to check it out, and discovered it was in fact a stolen one. All that occurred resulted from the many impulses we receive throughout our lives that connect to many people who are to become involved once the subconscious mind is obeying a clear emotional order. Did cousin Ivy know the policeman who informed her that her car had been found? Of course not, neither did her subconscious mind know those who were to assist in the finding of the car, thus proving that the world of the subconscious mind is also living a life like ours, but without the equipment we require to make contact of this nature.

In 1985 I wrote a manuscript which was unacceptable to the

publishers we sent it to, for various reasons which were explained to me when a woman associated with the publishers concerned called on me. When I had made the arrangements for this visit to take place, I desperately wanted two of the others who were aware of my findings to be present also. I telephoned the first one and she told me that, exactly as I had pointed out in my findings, she had wished for something and it had taken place – but she had worded her wish incorrectly. It appeared that a week or so previously she had attended a farewell party of a work colleague who was leaving. At this gathering she had said how she would love time off work for a spell without actually feeling ill. A short time after and in the course of her work she had in fact had an accident in which she had broken bones in both her feet. At the time I wanted her to attend the coming meeting she was off work sitting in a chair unable to walk, but not feeling unwell, just as she had wished.

I then phoned cousin Ivy and asked if she could come up from the coast and attend the meeting and give me support. Unfortunately she had agreed to spend ten days visiting a relative of hers and was due to leave on this trip on the very day the meeting was to take place. I then suggested that since she was not looking forward to going on the visit at this particular time, that we put my findings into practice, as we had a week for something to develop and cause her intended visit to be cancelled. She agreed, and we clearly stated that nothing bad like sickness would be the cause of the cancellation. The evening before the meeting was due to take place Ivy phoned to say that nothing had altered the arrangements and she was leaving early the following morning. Two days later I received another phone call from her to inform me that after many hours of stress and expense on the motorway she had to return home and cancel the visit. It appeared that while driving on the motorway her car developed a bad vibration that affected the steering. As soon as possible she left the motorway and found a garage to have it investigated. She was told by the mechanic that her steering column was causing the trouble and it could well be dangerous for her to continue her long journey. Very slowly she headed back for home. Once there she drove the car to her local garage to have the required repairs carried out. On collecting the car she was informed that the steering column was in perfect condition and the cause of the vibration was nothing more than the need for the wheels to be correctly balanced. So she too got her desire but had failed to state, 'In time to attend the meeting.'

These events just show how we go through life without relating and connecting everyday occurrences with our thoughts and desires. The two I have quoted, although alarming to those concerned, were neither as serious as they might have been. But had either of these cases been more serious, or even fatal, they would still have arisen from the mind while the subconscious mind was obeying instructions and not, as one would suppose, just one of life's hazards.

Throughout the writing of the previous manuscript and this more detailed and open version of my life, each time I write a chapter something takes place or is said relating to what I have so recently written. When I wrote for the first time early details of my life and I was writing about Billy Short, my sister Margie, on one of her Monday visits, produced a photo of my mother and asked if I recalled it. It was a photo taken in the very same shop where Billy, my brother and their friend had theirs taken, that he gave away in the air raid shelter. My mother had had this one taken in the same year.

On at least five occasions, although I am certainly not the type of person to write a book, I have been asked by different people, 'Why don't you write a book?' I was in a park on one of these occasions thinking of what I was writing, when a woman I hardly knew came from around the corner and said, 'Why don't you write a book and let me type it?'

I said, 'What on earth made you say that?'

To which she replied, 'I honestly don't know, I said it on impulse.'

On another occasion just a couple of days ago I said to a man I was talking to about gardening, 'I really must go. I have things to do.'

He replied, 'What are you doing, writing a book?'

The young relative whom I see so often speaks of things I have written and on one occasion she said to me, 'Do you think that we know something that no one else knows?' What could I say?

Now I want to relate something that took place just three

136

days before I began writing this account of it, on *Friday 9th May, 1986*. This particular young relative was born on 9th April and had been given a cassette player and radio with headphones by her mother for her birthday. On Friday she asked if I would give her money to buy new batteries for it, so I asked her first to help me in clearing out the drawer where I keep my stationery. I told her to throw away the stapler which was now over twenty years old and not working properly, and I would get a new smaller one. During the clearing out of the drawer I also told her that her mother had bought me the wrong-sized enveloped and I had a whole box of useless envelopes because I needed the long white ones. I asked her to remind me at the shops to buy a new reel of Sellotape. She then went to the shops and came back with her new batteries and sat trying out various tapes. She came over to me and said, 'What is this tape? Is it yours, because it is not mine.' I put on her headphones and could not believe what I was hearing. It was in fact a tape I had made of the visit of the mediums Mr and Mrs Sturd when they came to my home at Joan Wallis's request back in the early part of 1984.

I stated earlier that the whole evening had been a disaster. I felt that they had told me nothing, my friends were very angry as they had not been included and had sat the whole of the evening in my front room, and even the tape I had made had not come out. I rewound that tape the following morning and it was blank so I threw it into a drawer in disgust. Now here I was clearly listening to all that the mediums had said, confirming who they were and even recent parts of this book was on the tape spoken by me, confirming much of what I have written. On *Sunday 11th May, 1986* I took my young relative to a boot sale and the only items I purchased were, at bargain prices, long white envelopes, a stapler, and Sellotape all from different stalls and without realizing at the time of purchase they were each the very items I had mentioned I needed. Then I shuddered. On one of the stools was a box that contained a little silver spoon and eggcup, which I most certainly did not purchase. So you see how involved my life is with the subconscious world within.

In the case of my determination to purchase an electric fire, this was a very positive order to my subconscious mind, while all the events on a smaller scale, like the decision to go to that

137

particular café, the spotting of the man unloading his car and my speaking to him etc., were among the many impulses sent to the thinking mind to enable the command to be obeyed. Had not the man with the fire to sell made a positive decision the previous day to sell the fire, when he asked the man who gave me his phone number to buy it from him? And do you see, too, the involvement of a less important chain of events with apparently casual events of life? I did not want to install central heating; while the man wanted to sell the fire because he had central heating. The day that Ivy suggested I purchase such a fire was the same day that the man had made the effort to attempt to sell his, so that when I approached the man from the secondhand store the following day he was in a position to set up the meeting and so for both our desires to materialize. Why, too, a man from near my home in London?

I would like now to relate events that took place about six months before writing this. John always had a terrible fear of spiders, that towards the end of his life had become quite out of hand, and many of our phone calls during his spells at the coast consisted of details of how he had spent hours cleaning his accommodation, pulling out large pieces of furniture to ensure there were no spiders. When I saw a very large spider in my bath I immediately thought of what John's reaction would have been on seeing it. I could never bear the thought of a spider touching me but at the same time, unlike John, I never wish to kill a spider because of this. I decided to run the water tap and when the spider floated on top of the water I would scoop it on to a newspaper I had ready, and quickly run it out into the back garden. Because I had failed to put the plug in first, however, the spider ran to the far end of the bath out of reach of the water. I quickly unhooked the plug and chain from the shower button and accidentally turned the shower on. I was completely drenched. The spider, however, did float on the water but when I scooped it on to the newspaper it promptly ran towards my arm. In fear, I quickly shook it on to the floor, and then had no alternative but to tread on it and kill it as John would have done. Once I had recovered from the incident I thought to myself 'This is the kind of thing that connects to something else at a later date.'

About three days later I was unable to collect Joan as usual to take her to the club, so I met her there. She informed me that Dennis, her husband, was in great pain and had been for three days. He had actually cried with the pain from a twisted back, and was still lying in bed unable to move in spite of the pain killers the doctor had given him. I asked how he had hurt his back, and she went on to explain that while she was making the bed in the bedroom, Dennis was sitting in the bathroom on the edge of the bath with his legs inside it re-sealing the gap around the bath. Suddenly a large spider appeared in the bedroom and she screamed. Dennis had tried to get to her as quickly as possible to see what was wrong and had twisted his back in the process.

The following day Joan informed my young relative that one of her cats had been missing for a couple of days. The next day was one of the evenings I was to collect Joan to go to our club and feeling very tired I told my young relative I would have a little sleep in the chair while she watched children's television. Just as I closed my eyes she said to me, 'I wonder if Auntie Joan has found her cat?' I said I had no idea, and closed my eyes again. I thought to myself, 'I wonder if I could cure Dennis's bad back as I did with John,' but then forgot the idea since I realized that like John, Dennis did not go along with talk of such things, although Joan did. I fell asleep and was awakened about a half an hour later by the ringing of the telephone. It was Joan. She told me to tell my young relative that her cat had come back and said she had told Dennis how I had cured John's back several years previously and had begged him to allow her to ask me to do likewise for him. Finally he had agreed and she was now asking if I would. I told her I would call on her earlier than usual that evening and see Dennis before we left for the club.

When I arrived she took me upstairs to where Dennis was lying in bed at an angle facing the wall. Joan said she would go downstairs and get herself ready to go to the club. I asked Dennis if he could lie on his front, but he said he was unable to move from the position he was in, and told me near enough where the pain was. As I had with John, I gently moved my hands over the area and Dennis remarked how very hot my hands had become, and said it was the warmest his back had felt since Joan had placed a hot water bottle on it. After about three or four minutes I stopped and said to Dennis, 'Now get out of bed.'

He replied, 'You don't understand. I can't move and it took a long time to get into bed.'

I said, 'But that was before I came here, so now get out of bed.' I walked out of the bedroom on to the landing, then went back and looked into the room to see Dennis out of bed walking around. He said all he now had was just a twinge. The very words John had used. I said, 'Let's go downstairs and surprise Joan.' He said he would put his slippers on first and I offered to get them for him, but he insisted he could bend and put them on himself, which he did and then put on a dressing gown and we walked down the stairs to join Joan, who looked quite startled.

About four months before this event I had told Joan that I had broken my very large casserole dish and was looking out for a replacement, but had not been able to find the right kind of one I required. On the following club night Joan said to me, 'I don't really need this casserole dish of mine, would you like it?' I knew it was her way of discreetly thanking me and the dish she gave me was identical to the one I had broken. Now into this one story come several aspects of the power of the subconscious world: the fact that as we think of a person so we transmit thoughts back and forth, the repetition of small incidents linking with a more serious chain of events, thus causing vital connections. I believe that Joan merely made me the inspiration for Dennis to transmit his desire to his subconscious mind. I did not cure Dennis, his emotional desire did this. Joan received his transmitted thoughts and received an impulse to request my help in the very same way that cousin Ivy had when wishing for her car back. Joan's own subconscious mind, having received Dennis's transmitted desire, was sent an impulse to recall something I had told her a long time ago. All a complex mixture of the workings of the subconscious mind and its domination of the thinking mind in the process of obeying its master's orders.

I had been made aware that the whole of life formed a pattern instigated by the inner world and created by our emotional demands, and our beliefs.

During one of my sister Margie's recent visits she shocked me when she told me how my mother knew at our sister Beth's christening that she would die. I asked how she could possibly have known that. My sister replied that it was a well-known old

140

wives' tale that if a midwife was godmother to two children in the same year, the second one would die. At the christening of Beth the midwife whom my mother had chosen to be godmother had remarked, 'This is the second child I have been godmother to this year,' and from that moment mum knew Beth was going to die.

Now since nothing works for the good only, must we not understand that all emotional beliefs work also for the bad events of our lives also?

Only when all the implications of my findings are completely understood will anyone fully realize the unhappiness we ourselves create in our individual lives, affecting all those round us, and on a far greater scale affecting the whole world. When I mentioned in an earlier chapter the many mixed emotions that I experienced following the death of my friend Pat's grandchild (the cot death), how I had created havoc in my life, so too is the havoc existing on this earth created by man.

One day I decided to experiment further with my findings, and made it known that I could read people's minds. I was not taken too seriously until even I was shocked as to what I was able to reveal to those who came forward to prove me wrong. When complete strangers approached me to have their minds read because of my success, and the irate parents of a teenager demanded to know who had been telling me their personal affairs, I promptly called a halt to the whole thing. How could I have possibly have told the parents that their son had transmitted it all to me while I had merely cleared my mind to accept his transmitted thoughts?

During that period I was introduced to a young woman who had very recently lost her father. I asked her not to say one word to me and I would tell her many details concerning her father. I described what her father had looked like prior to his illness, the kind of man he was, where he had kept his private documents and what was found among these documents, which before his death no one had know existed. It was all correct in every detail. Now this poor woman was so convinced that her father had contacted me and given me all these details that I found it impossible to convince her that I was not a medium, or in touch with her dead father. Neither could I reveal my findings to her, so although she lived quite a distance away I received telephone calls from her trying to get me to give further details concerning other relatives. What a hopeless situation, since I had merely carried out the very same procedure as I had when reading minds. She, being in an emotional state having so recently lost her father, transmitted all the relevant details to me. I, being a good receiver, repeated what I had extracted from her subconscious mind. All the thoughts transmitted by a person when alive remain in the subconscious minds of family and friends and may be transmitted to a medium or some other sensitive, long after death of the person has taken place. Did John not transmit his secrets to me in the form of a compulsive daydream? Surely John not only transmitted this to me throughout our life together, he transmitted constantly, and now he is dead does not all that he transmitted live on in my subconscious mind? During my long search for the truth I often claimed that if a medium could tell me something only *I* knew, then I would believe. This offer certainly does not hold good now.

Whether a mind reader, fortune teller or medium, the procedure is exactly the same. The client transmits and the one with so-called special powers receives. When these people speak of the spirit world they are indeed correct, there is a spirit world but it is one and the same spirit world that I speak of, the *world of the subconscious mind*. Because these people, like myself, have quite accidentally been able to penetrate the subconscious world in various ways, they presume quite understandably that it is from the next world that their knowledge arises, and being showmen, so to speak, add so much that is certainly not so, to make their claims more convincing. Could I not have said to the young woman who had lost her father, 'Yes, I have your father here and he is telling me where he keeps his belongings, etc.'?

Yet another test I made concerned cousin Ivy once again. During a telephone conversation, she being an artist had informed me that she had painted five new pictures. I suggested that she visualized each one separately and I would attempt to receive from her mind details of each picture. This I did correctly in each case. By staring at the wall I was able to view in great detail the picture she had in mind, proving that we also transmit visions. At a later date I was also able to prove that apart from the thoughts we transmit we also transmit our moods, whether anger, or happiness, once the connection is made. This finding was to show what had taken place when I was in John's company and felt unnecessarily aggressive.

12

Several times during my long search for the truth I spoke to a number of people who had actually seen the ghost of a loved one a few months or even a year after they had died. Each was so sincere that although I had never experienced anything supernatural in the whole of my life, I had no reason to doubt their stories any more than they could dispute what I claimed to have occurred to me. In fact, I was always very interested and would want to know all the details. One such woman, who had seen her late mother standing beside her bed smiling at her before disappearing, was obviously very disturbed by the experience. She said she had never previously believed in ghosts, but since she had seen her mother so clearly no one could say anything to convince her it had not happened. I asked her how her mother had died and she told me that she had been ill for some time. She went on to say how happy her mother seemed when she appeared, looking as she had before her illness.

I also recalled a young man who told me a very similar story except that his mother had died suddenly. He was very open and told everyone he met how he had seen his mother after her death. She appeared to him in the hallway of their home. He attended as many spiritualist meetings as possible in the hope of receiving a message from her. I asked him if she looked as she did before her death, and he too replied she was much younger, more agile looking and very happy. At the time of asking these questions I could not make out why it was so important to know how their mothers had looked during the visitation. Now it has become clear why I had to ask this question.

As I have said, the subconscious mind not only has the power to transmit and receive thoughts, to go into the past and the future, and even transfer our thoughts into the making of other people's dreams, it has many other abilities including the power to project our emotional desires into images. Just as we project a film on a screen, so the subconscious mind can project thoughts in picture form to be seen. This can occur when someone is under the kind of emotional stress that a death in the family would cause. The natural desire to see the loved one again is given as an emotionally charged order to the subconscious mind, which is obeyed. But while desiring to see their loved one again, the thinking mind would wish to remember them not as ill or suffering but well and happy. This is the image the thinker prefers to print on their mind, and thus they automatically convey this picture to the subconscious mind when desiring to see the loved one again. The subconscious obeys the command and projects the ghost at the desired stage of life. No one would wish to see a loved one in the final stages of life, or the body as they may have seen it once death had taken place. This indicates that the vision originated in the mind of the person who was experiencing the sighting. It is this memory and picture of a loved one that is transferred to the mind of a medium when a sitting is in progress, along with other knowledge the medium may have the gift to extract from the subconscious mind of those present.

How many mediums would accept a challenge to repeat all his or her claims with the use of a truth drug or a lie detector as I would willingly do? Even the atmosphere built up before a spiritualist meeting helps arouse the emotions of those who are to take part, and an emotional person is in the correct state to have much information extracted from them. Details of the death of a loved one are easier than other subjects, as the person desiring to contact a loved one automatically relives emotions that took place when the death occurred, and it is these very strong feelings that will allow many strange events to take place on these occasions. Even the emotional desire of the medium and all who take part play a role in making some bizarre events take place. If all that has happened in my life was the result of only my desires, then imagine the power aroused when several people desire the same kind of experience.

I had often wondered why the pathetic messages from the

spirit world that mediums claim to be in contact with always related to our world, and usually never described the world in which they were now living. This is because all that is abstracted from the client's subconscious mind did in fact take place in our world prior to death having taken place.

We are all aware that once a person dies, the spirit leaves the body, but no one can say where the spirit goes, because this information is in no living mind and therefore cannot be extracted by a medium or the like. We all know for certain that the body is either cremated or rots beneath the ground. So we have positive proof that the body is destroyed after death takes place. Yet when a person claims to have seen a ghost it is not of the departed spirit but of the now destroyed body, once again indicating that it is a vision of their thoughts they see, projected by the subconscious mind. Nothing comes from the dead: only from the living.

Let us consider an historic building which is reputed to be haunted by a figure from the past, where the ghost of a woman has been seen on various occasions by many people. The chain of events for this would have started at the time of the woman's death. A relative or close associate who knew her in life would have had a sighting of her after death because of an emotional desire to do so. The knowledge of what took place would be made known to others, who then also receive a transmitted vision of the dead woman. This is all kept alive by transmission of thoughts from one generation to the next keeping the story going. Others in turn would build up within themselves a feeling of apprehension and fear when visiting the building and knowing of its reputation and details of the said ghost, would also project the very same vision as those in the past had done, thus making the story even more authentic. Since only people in an extreme frame of mind are likely to project this subconscious picture into an actual vision, only a very few people really see the ghost. All details have merely been transmitted from subconscious to subconscious throughout the years.

We can apply the same basic principle to a building visited by someone who does not know of its reputation for being haunted and yet still sees a ghost. Since all old buildings have an atmosphere, sometimes a visitor will have a great desire to know of its past. The subconscious mind accepts this command and then contacts the subconscious of one who knows the answers in the very same way all my desires had been answered. The knowledgeable one then transmits this information along with details of the so-called ghost and the vision can be projected again. This is all, as I have said, from a living brain and not from the dead.

Nothing comes from the dead, only from the living. Thoughts transferred from someone dead will, however, be alive in the mind of a close relative and these too may be raised in such a way that it is assumed they could only have come from the other side, as mediums like us to believe.

While I do not doubt the sincerity of clairvoyants, mediums, fortune tellers and the like, I do dispute where their knowledge comes from. I fully understand their misguided belief that it comes from those who have died. We only have to ask, if they are in contact with the next world, why are they not aware of the life hereafter? Also why aren't the many murders which are committed solved by simply contacting the victim and asking who committed the crime? The reason they cannot reveal these facts is because they are dead, just as information about the 'hereafter' is not on any living subconscious mind.

We have all heard of a medium assisting the police to find a missing murder victim. The medium may have taken the police to a remote spot where the body was buried, but they still did not contact the victim. That is impossible. What they did do, however, was to contact subconsciously the mind of the murderer. He, or she, alone could transmit the thoughts, the scene and even the name of the place where the victim was buried. All as my way of life has proven. The world would be void of crime if the claims of mediums and others were true. Every so-called mystery that has occurred since time began, originated with the powers of the world of the subconscious mind. How can one explanation cover so many phenomena and still be doubted as the true answer?

Remember, we are not supposed to be aware of the subconscious world. Because of this, only a minority of the world's population experiences unusual events and phenomena. Everyone, however, is aware of the many times during the course of normal life when there is reason to say: 'If I had not done this . . . then . . .', or 'If I had not done that . . .

perhaps'. 'If I had kept the appointment ... then ...' IF, IF, IF again and again. Our whole lives are affected by the word IF, and yet the IFs of our lives are all part of the subconscious mind, which is in the process of obeying its orders, whether they be trivial or important. Indeed, the subconscious mind created the IFs of our life as I shall now reveal by taking just three chains of events from a daily diary that I kept for a few months last summer when wishing to verify my findings. All that I am about to write was clearly obvious to me, yet one woman who witnessed the whole of one chain of events made no comment whatsoever with regards to its strangeness, which shows just how differently we think and how our minds have different priorities. Remember that I claim that if we intend to see someone we think of them and our thoughts then relate to what is transmitted and received once the connection has been made; also how a dear wish is granted via another person receiving impulses. And how our dreams do not belong to us. I will now relate a conversation which took place last summer in a park. Madge and I were talking.

Madge	I had a strange dream last night.
Me	Tell me about it, I am interested in dreams.
Madge	I dreamt that Kelly's cat had got into my flat and gone into a rage and was attacking a huge tin of corned beef in my cupboard. I picked the cat up and threw it out of the door, but it came back again and again and I was in a state of hitting it on the back trying to get rid of it. Then Kelly's mother came to my door and took the cat away. By the way, did you hear anything about a house that caught fire last night?
Me	No, where was it?
Madge	Well I heard that it was not far from here and that an elderly lady died in the fire, I would like to find out more about it.

(Kelly comes and joins us. She is twelve years old.)

Kelly	Something is wrong with our cat. It has hurt its back and my mother is going to take it to the vet.

I laugh to myself, because I thought, 'Madge did that when she hit it in her dream.'

(We are now joined by a woman walking her dog, whom we vaguely know.)

Woman	You all seem to be deeply engrossed in something.
Me	Madge has just been telling me a strange dream she had.
Woman	I had a very strange and frightening dream last night too. I dreamt that one of my cats was staggering around the floor and was dying, and then it lay still. I picked it up and it had turned very strange as though it were flat and had no inside. I awoke quite upset about the dream. I went back to sleep again and in my dream I could hear voices shouting and yelling. I then woke up and realized I was not dreaming, and I jumped out of bed and ran to the window and saw that the house opposite was on fire. An old lady died in the fire and her cat died with her, the fireman buried it in her front garden.
Madge	Where do you live? I wondered where the fire was.
Me (to the woman)	What have you done to your finger? (It was heavily bandaged).
Woman	I cut it very badly opening a tin of corned beef.

That evening when I picked up Joan for the club she told me that for a quick meal she had opened a tin of corned beef.

The following day, being Monday, my sister Margie called as usual and also my sister Winnie (Bill's wife) and they were talking about Bill's death. Margie then said, 'I shall never forget the night you called to say that mum had died. I had just had a corned beef sandwich for supper when you rang the bell.'

I was taking Margie home in my car a week or so later and as we passed a certain road she said, 'I shall never forget how we had an accident in our car there,' meaning she and her husband. She went on to say that they were not hurt but when she got home she found that one of the lenses had fallen out of her glasses. She said to me, 'Guess where I found it?'

149

I said, 'In your coat pocket.'

To which she said, 'Yes.'

That evening I went to my club as I usually do, on arriving I took off my coat and laid it across the next table to save it for two women who sit there. They came in and thanked me and passed me my coat. Then the one who handed me my coat said, 'Ooha.' I asked what was wrong and she said one of the lenses had fallen out of her glasses. One week later a lens fell out of my glasses also, after having laid my coat across the table once again.

Prior to my findings having been revealed to me I would never even have conceded the idea of any association whatsoever with these very minor chains of events, but do you now see how they do in fact link up with serious events of life also, such as the death of the woman in the fire? And do you see how our dreams, like our thoughts, are also shared with other people? Because of yet other chains I also discovered that not only do we transmit our thoughts but our conditions and frame of mind too, and this is what John had been doing to me when we were working together. I will give a brief account of this by describing another chain of events.

One Monday just before Margie was due to pay me her usual visit, I suddenly felt very cold and turned my fire full on, although the room never required the fire to be on full. At that moment my doorbell rang and Margie said on entering, 'I am absolutely frozen.' Yet she found my room too warm and asked if I would lower the fire. She then went on to say how she hated to go to her friend's house because she turns off all the heating after a short time of it being on. Then she informed me that our sister Winnie was also calling today. At that moment the doorbell rang and I went to let Winnie in.

I said, 'Hasn't it turned cold today?'

She replied, 'Yes, my heating had only been on a short time and I turned it off, thinking it was warmer.'

She entered the room and said to Margie, 'I was thinking about you as I rang, and wondered if you were here yet.' (Before Margie had arrived I was having my bath when I realized that I had a huge bruise on the top of my leg where I had knocked myself the day before.)

Margie then said, 'I knocked my leg on the way here and I bet I will get a big bruise.'

Can you see how individually each and every comment and action we make means absolutely nothing on a separate basis, but collectively they give an entirely different picture?

How very, very clever the inner world is, so constructed that we are so utterly unaware of it. And we must understand that the one who gave us the subconscious also gave us our body and thinking mind. I imagine that my childhood thoughts that those who died had returned to where they came from, reflected the fact that when the body is dead the subconscious mind returns, and it is only then the provider of the tools inspects how we used them.

If so much can happen in one person's life resulting from strong desires, then what happens in all those religions where so many people have been raised in staunch, or even fanatical, beliefs? I realize that most religions speak of a better life after death and thinking along this line I can see why believers have died in their millions, from starvation, holy wars and other horrors. Were not their subconscious minds obeying them too? We have many different religions and perhaps it is in those areas where people are not so fanatical that there are lesser sized tragedies, such as plane disasters, train crashes, traffic pile-ups. These are not disasters on a national scale but more local, bringing together people who had either intentionally or accidentally desired the afterlife. You will hear many times of the person who did not board the plane after all, or of the one who took their place at the last moment. And the accident happens. Was this the subconscious world completing many final puzzles, with just one last piece?

When a country declares war on another, the invaded country may accept that defeat is inevitable and therefore it becomes so. But the invader eventually must also become a victim at a later time. No empire has ever survived because it arose in blood. Religions which have survived do so because they are essentially based on good. All that happens to an individual also applies in the larger chains of events that involve communities and nations.

When someone prays and the prayers are answered, what is really happening is that thoughts are transferred from the one praying to the one being prayed for. This assists in making the desire a reality in the same way I assisted cousin Ivy to recover her stolen car, and Joan's husband Dennis to be cured of his back, and John also. Had they not each asked for my help? But it cannot happen if the subject of the prayers does not wish for help. At the same time as we pray for another we are also praying for ourselves. All we desire for another must eventually happen to us. The 'power of prayer' is really the power of the subconscious, carrying out its orders. During the war when very young I had often wondered how both the English soldiers and the German soldiers fighting the same battle could pray to the same God. Now I understand.

Why did I receive knowledge of the future in the form of a story and not as the bare facts of John's intentions? This question makes me think of the Bible and all the other holy books and the many stories they contain. Like my findings, is the same message repeated in different ways to enable a clearer understanding with only the appearance of contradiction?

The different sexes on earth exist for the purpose of reproduction in this world and therefore in the world of the subconscious also. Throughout time man has felt superior to his female counterpart, but this is not so in the world of the subconscious, being of spirit and not body. The instructions in the Bible were for everyone to spread chains of goodness throughout the world. We are all meant to be priests and ministers of good, instructing and guiding others, not just the chosen few as selected by religious sects via the thinking mind of man. Even a car battery will not work without negative and positive terminals, but neither is of more importance than the other. What is important is that the car will start up, but although we can see the engine working we cannot see the power that comes from the battery, no more than we can see the power of the subconscious mind whether via a male or female. Neither can male or female reproduce without the other. I know that I could never ever belong to a religious sect again. I do not need to be part of the dividing line that man has created in the spiritual world of religion. However, I do accept that churches are meeting places which enable all those desiring to congregate to make more powerful their desires in life.

13

A short time ago I saw a programme on television called 'The Silent Twins'. This programme told the bizarre story of June and Jennifer Gibbons, identical twin daughters of an RAF serviceman from Barbados and his wife. Although they had an elder brother and sister they grew up in their own private world, only speaking to one another. Throughout their school life they refused to acknowledge the outside world, defying all attempts to get through to them, and protecting one another against the hostility they attracted from other children. Yet each twin would also receive the full brunt of the other's anger, resulting in terrible quarrels between them.

At sixteen, after leaving a special school, they shut themselves in their bedroom, taking refuge in their mutual fantasy world. Here they acted out fantasy games with dolls and soon began writing novels, which grew out of stories they had written for the dolls. Writing became an obsession they took very seriously, sending away for a writing course and reading everything they could lay their hands on. But their ambition to become famous authors failed, and they fell under the influence of three American brothers, acting out their fantasies in real life, discovering sex and drugs and turning to stealing, vandalism and arson, for which they have now been committed indefinitely to Broadmoor special hospital.

Marjorie Wallace, a writer who has visited them regularly and studied their diaries and writings, recently published a book about them, on which the television programme I saw was based. Marjorie Wallace describes them as 'two human beings who love and hate each other with such intensity that they can neither live together nor apart.' She concludes that 'The mystery of the silent twins . . . is really the story of a mystic bondage by which the extremes of good and evil, which they both personify, have led to the possession of one twin by another. It is also about the waging of a silent war – which neither can win – the struggle for individuality . . .' If the account of these twins is accurate, I would like to show how easy it is to understand why they act as they do.

I now realize that when we moved from the East End of London, around the time of my ninth birthday was when all the strange events began in my life. And this was in fact the time I had 'come of age' in the world of the subconscious and could now issue my own emotional orders. In the case of the silent twins it appears that they began to act strangely at the age of ten, when they too would have 'come of age' in the world of the subconscious. Why the twins are as they are, and all the conflict that goes on between them stems from an accident of nature. Just as a child may be born crippled, deformed or blind in an obvious way that we are able to see and understand, and in the same way that Siamese twins are born joined together, these unfortunate children were born sharing the same subconscious mind. Two bodies, two thinking minds and just one subconscious. The impulses they receive are one and the same and cause them to behave and talk identically to each other even when they are physically parted. They cannot be separated spiritually. If a child acted as they did and refused to speak and walked alone, or held her arm in a certain way, no doctor would claim to be baffled by this behaviour, but because in the case of the twins there are two of them doing the same as each other, then doctors are baffled.

When we are in the process of deciding to carry out a certain act we may as well be in two minds before acting or, having done something not very nice, we try mentally to justify our actions. The twins, having two bodies and just one spirit, direct this kind of conflict at each other. Because they do not know why they are different so the conflict goes on, and while they cannot live with each other, they cannot exist apart either. What in fact they are doing is the same as if my left arm blamed my right arm for all that was occurring in my life. In their case they are directing their anger at another entire being. It was asked on the programme, 'What strange power dominates their lives?' I suggest it is the same power that

154

dominates everyone's life, in many strange ways.

Regression too is clear to me now. I have drawn a chart showing how thoughts are transmitted from a mother to her children and grandchildren and I am aware that the thought chain does not begin with our immediate family but comes through from our ancestors. The hypnotist raises transmitted thoughts, not only pertaining to the life of the person being regressed; he also transmits his own immediate thoughts which may well be dwelling on the period of time he is asking his subject to go back to, and of which he may well have considerable knowledge.

So complicated is the world of the subconscious mind that every aspect of its ability is almost inconceivable to the thinking mind and the world we are aware of. Yet, like the many chains that link up before an event can be finalized, so we are inextricably linked to the world within us with an important role in the operation: giving the 'master's orders' to the subconscious, which must obey.

We are all aware of the curses made by witch doctors or found in such places as ancient Egyptian tombs. These too are created by fear, a fear that has been passed from living minds to the subconscious throughout the ages. Each death makes the curse more authentic. An explorer may brush aside the story of the curse but will subconsciously believe in it when another less convinced associate does in fact die. He too becomes an unwilling victim a little later and so the chain continues through the ages, kept alive by the living mind. Once again the origin is with emotions and belief. The victim of a witch doctor's curse reacts in the same way because he believes the witch doctor has special powers. The witch doctor does indeed have such powers, but so too does the victim.

I also believe that in many cases people who fear greatly a certain happening such as mugging, rape, robbery and even murder, may cause themselves to become such victims by contacting the mugger, the rapist, the thief or the murderer in the same way I came into contact with the man who sold us the faulty property and he with me. Fear is such a strong emotion it can command the subconscious. Similarly, anything that happens for a good reason must also happen exactly the same for a bad one, otherwise we will be back to giving God the credit for all the good things and blaming man for all the

MOTHER

TRANSMITTED THOUGHTS TO

CHILD   CHILD   CHILD   3 children

TRANSMITTED THOUGHTS TO

CHILD CHILD CHILD CHILD CHILD CHILD 6 grandchildren

TRANSMITTED THOUGHTS TO

CHILD CHILD CHILD CHILD CHILD CHILD CHILD CHILD CHILD CHILD CHILD CHILD 12 great grandchildren

MOTHER (NOW GREAT GRANDMOTHER) DIES

TRANSMITTED THOUGHTS LIVE ON IN SUBCONSCIOUS MINDS OF HER CHILDREN, GRANDCHILDREN AND GREATGRANDCHILDREN

HER CHILDREN DIE. TRANSMITTED THOUGHTS LIVE ON IN HER GRANDCHILDREN AND GREATGRANDCHILDREN

HER GRANDCHILDREN DIE. TRANSMITTED THOUGHTS LIVE ON IN HER GREATGRANDCHILDREN

THE LAST SURVIVOR AMONG HER GREATGRANDCHILDREN DIES: **SHE IS FINALLY DEAD** bad.

The subconscious mind of an intended murderer must, before the event, be informed of the desire to kill. Every killing is connected with some kind of emotion, whether it be hate, vengeance or even pleasure. Once the subconscious has been instructed, it then contacts the subconscious of a likely victim among those who have, through fear, made themselves eligible. Many impulses are set into motion and the fateful meeting takes place, having been arranged. Once the murder has been committed, the murderer's subconscious must also arrange an eventual bad death for its master, since all commands must be obeyed. Although the subconscious has assisted in finding the victim it will not finalize the event until the master has been obeyed completely. The same goes for a good deed. The one who saves a life will, during the course of his or her own life, also be saved by another. It is as the Bible says, 'Do as you would be done by.'

Everyone lives the life that they have themselves created, whether in riches, poverty, happiness or misery.

If you, the reader, can now understand why and how all was to take place in my life and accept my findings as so, it must be borne in mind that it is not possible to select only what you wish to believe and dismiss the remainder as an unexplained mystery, to maintain the delight we all get when hearing a ghost story or seeing a thriller on television. Even a strange event of your own life that you may well have related on many occasions will no longer retain the same air of intrigue it once had. Or the amazing sitting you may have had with a medium, fortune teller or clairvoyant will no longer be an awe-inspiring conversation. The very fact that my findings explain and dismiss communication with those now departed will naturally be resented by many people for obvious reasons. Those who believed that it was the spirit of a loved one they saw, will not want to believe that the vision arose from their own subconscious mind. But let us return to the ghost or vision. Doesn't a weary thirsty traveller in the desert visualize and crave to see an oasis? Isn't this also a vision projected from his subconscious called an hallucination? Why do we accept in the first instance that a ghost is of unearthly origin and the oasis an hallucination? They are both produced by the same process.

We all get a thrill out of telling or hearing a ghost story, or seeing a good mystery on television, and would not wish for this element of life to disappear. Yet, once fully understood, my findings of the truth are a hundred times more alarming than the creepiest of ghost stories. When each of you realizes that every thought and great desire, good or bad, that you may have in the private world of your thinking mind affects all those around you, only then will you understand the full importance of all I am trying to reveal. When as a child I was taught that God was everywhere and knew and saw all we did, and we would be punished for all the wrong we did, I lived in terror. Now I understand how this comes about, since our subconscious mind repays all our deeds good or bad. So once again I am as I was long ago, fearing every bad thought.

As we get older nature itself calms our emotions and we desire less and less from life. This is nature's way of lessening the amount of pieces of puzzle being added to our mountain yet to be completed. We mellow in our old age. I, too, apart from the knowledge I have of my life, desire very little other than what I now have, and lead as uncomplicated a life as is possible. However, I still experience events ahead of the time we would normally become aware of them, and I am now aware, because our lives are led on this basis, that I shall continue to do so until the time of my death.

Early one morning when in the process of writing the first manuscript, I was struggling mentally to bring every aspect of my findings together to be able to present them in the clearest way possible. I was trying to form a mental picture to enable me to do this. Suddenly for no apparent reason I became extremely tired. So much so that I sat back in my chair and closed my eyes. As I did so a very strange thing occurred, something I had never experienced before. It was as though I had left my body and was looking down on the earth from a very great height. I could see many, many circles, all intermingled but each a complete circle, and each I knew represented chains of events going back and forward throughout time. Parts of some chains were long since past, some were in the present, and some were yet to come years in the future. In what could have been no more than a couple of seconds, it was all over and I felt wide awake. I knew at that moment I had been looking down on one vast superbly

158

created *electrical communication system.* A whole new range of thoughts now dominated my mind and I knew that man and every living creature was part of this electrical creation. I thought 'If someone were to pull the plug out then every one of them would die.'

I was quite excited by what had taken place and mentally began to compare it with many aspects of life: all fitted perfectly into the scene I had glimpsed. I then thought on these lines: The earth is a circle and life too contains many chains. We have chains of thought, chains of circumstances, chain reactions concerning political views, religions, evil deeds and acts of love. Almost everything in life began in just one place, from fashions to the meals we eat, right up to the important things in life, and set up a chain reaction around the world. Very similar to the 'event' chains around my life that were happening on a higher plane. I then recalled how my findings had revealed that we transmit our thoughts, receive transmitted thought, project our thoughts, receive impulses and all the other abilities that my life has proved to me that the subconscious has the power to do. Does this not all relate to an electrical system? How, I asked myself, does this vast electrical system work and where does its energy source come from? I reasoned with myself that no electrical appliance could function without electricity. The answer to this question flowed into my mind. Man himself. Without our brain cells being charged by electricity from the body, man cannot survive, and since the subconscious also originates from the brain of man, we serve two existences at one and the same time. Neither can man survive without water. Water, as we know, generates electricity. The magnetism of the earth and the body also are of great importance to man and the collective world of the subconscious.

Following this experience I telephoned cousin Ivy and told her the whole story as I have written it and waited for her reaction. There was silence at the other end of the phone and I asked if she had grasped all I had revealed to her. 'Yes, I think so,' she replied in an uncertain tone.

'Then repeat to me what I saw when looking down from a great height,' I said.

'Well,' she replied, 'you saw all circles and they were coming up towards you and going off behind you.'

'No,' I said, knowing Ivy to be far more intelligent than this. 'The circles were around the earth, the creator of the earth was behind me,' meaning in the heavens.

'What a pity,' she replied, 'that you could not have found enough energy to turn around and look.'

Without thinking, I made a compulsive indignant reply: 'I could not do that, I would have to die first.'

'My God,' she said. 'Now I see the whole picture and it has blown my mind.' I apologized to her for my sharp reply and she said, 'Without it, I would have understood nothing.' Now cousin Ivy, like myself, is not a religious person, so apart from being shocked by my reply to her, I was also shocked by the impact my words had on her.

To me the implications of my findings are enormous. I can see how the pattern of our lives created by the world of the subconscious can be likened to the complex but orderly fashion of the whole universe. Before 1984 I had often marvelled at how Hitler, just one man, could wreak such devastation throughout the world. Now I understand. He simply transmitted his evil desires to those around him, and they in turn to many other people, thus creating the same effect that an atom bomb creates when splitting atoms into an ever-expanding circular chain reaction. Because these transmitted thoughts were unspoken, even intelligent and respectful citizens actually believed they arose from their own minds. And so because of this, Hitler was able to influence people from every walk of life and status. The greatest mistake we all make is believing the thoughts we think to be our own, the words we speak originate from our own minds, and the dreams we have relate only to our own lives. NOTHING BELONGS TO US ALONE. We are nothing more than electrical power houses, receiving and transmitting impulses constantly throughout our lives. Only our emotional demands are of our own making, and these desires plug us, so to speak, into the circuit that will eventually make our desires a reality.

14

January 1990

Six years have now passed since my findings were revealed to me, and four since the writing of the previous thirteen chapters of this manuscript during which time, because of new, or repeated experiences I have acquired a deeper understanding about the subconscious and its many natural abilities to carry out its complex relationship with the conscious mind.

Never once during this time has anything taken place to dispute my findings, but much had happened to confirm them.

I now intend carrying on with my writing and in the following chapters will include my new-found knowledge about various subjects. In this chapter I would like to discuss *special dreams.*

Special dreams being those I knew on awakening to be different from the average dream which consists of a mixture of daily events presented in an absurd manner, and which can so easily be accounted for. Even so, special dreams also contain daily happenings yet all fits in so perfectly with the storyline created by the subconscious. It is because of this that I shall include certain daily activities prior to the telling of a special dream.

In 1987 I had a whole series of special dreams all within a very short period of time. Because they occurred so closely together I was able to investigate them on a deeper level than ever before. Whereas, in the past, such dreams had caused concern, now, with my findings in mind I was able to understand so easily how each came about so it was a deeper understanding about them I now required.

I will begin by describing several special dreams and show how I arrived at certain conclusions.

Dream 1

I can hardly call this a dream because when I awakened from it I could remember nothing of the dream itself, only a very clear picture of the head and shoulders of a bearded policeman facing me. The following morning I had cause to go out early and, whilst driving along the deserted main road I decided to stop at the next newsagent and buy a newspaper. As I pulled up outside a newsagents so a police car sped up and came to a halt just in front of me. I saw a policeman leave the car and walk towards the shop and I followed him. He opened the shop door and seeing me, held it open for me to enter first. He was a bearded man and his face was identical to the policeman's in my dream.

Dream 2

At the time of having this dream I used to go to a Cash & Carry shop about six miles or so from my home every other week.

One Wednesday evening I had gone to bed early with a sickly headache I'd had for several days and had been unable to shake off. In my dream that night I found myself driving towards the Cash & Carry shop and was about half-way there. I was heading towards the end of a road which had a small island at the end. I was due to turn left by passing the island on the left side, but on impulse decided to turn left by going round the right side of the island, which meant I would be driving towards oncoming traffic turning into the road. I cut across the road and as I reached the island a large truck came around the corner and had to pull up because my car was in the way. This left a small gap between the truck and my car and to my horror a rag-and-bone man on a horse and cart began making his way towards the small gap with the intention of squeezing through. His horse's head was coming towards my open window. I was terrified so I jumped out of my car and ran behind it when I heard someone say, 'Hello,' as though they knew me. I looked up at the rag-and-bone man and he was smiling. I turned away and when I looked again I saw it was the owner of the Cash & Carry shop sitting on the horse and cart. I then woke up.

The next day, in spite of still having a headache I kept my regular hairdressing appointment although I did not feel like chatting whilst having my hair done. Not even when the hairdresser produced a book on the meaning of dreams.

Once back at home I made myself a cup of tea but decided I would rather be outside getting fresh air so I left the tea and took out my broom with the intention of sweeping the front garden. I had been out in the garden no more than a minute or so when I heard someone say, 'Hello'. I looked up and there was a rag-and-bone man sitting on his horse and cart by the kerb outside my front wall. I immediately recognized him as the man John and I used to save scrap metal for when we had our building company. He would give my daughters a ride on his horse and cart. He asked how the girls were and then asked what John was doing these days. He was shocked when he learned that John had been dead for five years. As he drove away I thought how unusual it was that he still used a horse and cart when most scrap dealers now used trucks. Believing this to be the reason for my dream I forgot all about it until three or four months later when driving to the Cash & Carry shop on one of my usual trips. On arriving at the spot where the rag-and-bone man had been in my dream, I thought to myself, 'That's where the horse and cart was'. On turning left I forgot the sudden thought. However, on the way home I had to remain in the middle of the road for several minutes before turning into the road with the island because a rag-and-bone man on a horse and cart was blocking the entry.

Dream 3

A relative asked if I would assist her in repapering her large lounge. She said it was prepared and painted and because she had only one day off work wondered if we could complete the task in one day. Because it was my club evening, I hoped we could complete by 5 pm. I suggested we worked round the room and left the chimney breast until last. This we did, and completed the papering of the chimney breast at 5 pm. In my club that evening I sat talking with a friend who was quite put out because her brother and his wife had insisted that she put them both up for two months whilst her brother was on a course in London. Their home being too far away for him to travel back and forth. They had even suggested that it would be better if they slept in her bedroom and she used the smaller one with a single bed.

I was quite exhausted that night when I went to bed and immediately fell into a deep sleep. In the dream that followed I found myself in a moonlit bedroom looking down on a man and a woman sleeping in what I knew to be my bed. Even thought it was a strange house I felt it was mine. I thought, 'I will have to find the room with a single bed and sleep there'. I turned and walked out of the room and found myself groping along a dark passageway. In spite of the darkness I became aware that everything around me was filthy dirty. When I spotted light coming from an open doorway to the right of the passage I made my way along and looked in. The room was also lit up by the moonlight coming in from a window behind the open door. I gasped with fright when I realized I was looking into my own lounge and that the large chimney breast had no wallpaper on it, although the rest of the room was in order. Wanting to get away from the room I continued on along the dark passage until I came to a door. I thought, 'This must be the room I am looking for', and I opened the door.

The room was lit by the moon shining in through a smallish bay window ahead of me. It had dirty torn curtains hanging from it held up by pieces of string. To the right I could clearly see a single bed with a dirty crumpled duvet lying down the centre. I made my way forward with the intention of trying to draw the curtains before getting into bed, when suddenly I stopped and looked down on the bed and to my horror I could see a bony elbow sticking out the side of the duvet. I put my hands to my mouth and said, 'Oh my God, it's dad'. (My father died of cancer in 1954). Then I thought, 'No, it's too short to be dad, it must be Kevin'. Fearing the body would try to get off the bed I bent over and pushed both my hands onto

164

the legs and began shouting for help. Sheer terror took over when I tried to remove my hands but found them firmly gripped between the bony knees of the body beneath the cover. Desperately trying to free my hands I began screaming. It was at this point I awoke to find myself lying on my side with my hands between my own knees.

Although it was only 4.15 am the dream had so unnerved me that I decided to get up rather than trying to go back to sleep. Whilst I sat drinking tea and going over the nightmare in my mind, I had a sudden impulse to check the date. On doing so I realized it was the second anniversary of Kevin's death that very morning.

Kevin was a drug addict. He died of an overdose just after 4 am in a large house used as a squat by such people. A few months prior to his death Kevin approached me and asked if I would help him to find somewhere where his addiction could be cured. After several weeks and many telephone calls I finally got an appointment to take him to a drug centre in London. He told the woman taking the interview how desperate he was for help and said that he was having to sleep in parks and squats because there was nowhere for him to go. He begged her for help, but she told him there were many others like him, and all she could do was give him an address in Knightsbridge where he would be given free soup. When a report of his inquest appeared in our local paper it was headed 'If only members of the public would help these youngsters'.

Kevin told his friends how I had tried to help him and this was the reason they tried to find me to tell me the sad news on the day of his death.

Dream 4

Because extensive work was being carried out on my house I had been working very hard from early morning until very late each night throughout the week. By Friday I was so exhausted that I went to bed at 8.30 pm and fell into a deep sleep the moment my head touched the pillow. I awakened around 1 am and heard a relative turn off the television and close her bedroom door. I drifted back to sleep. In the dream that followed I had awakened from sleep and found myself lying in the bedroom in which I had slept just after the war when I was seventeen years old. The bedroom curtains were open and a full moon was lighting up the room. My single bed was alongside the window as it had been at that time, but when I looked across the room to where my sisters Winnie and Margie had slept in a double bed, all I could see was a television set standing in the corner. Although our house had no electricity installed at that time and I was aware of this fact whilst lying there, it did not strike me as being strange. Everything felt quite normal as I gazed around the room until I looked up at the window and felt panic-stricken when I suddenly believed that John, my late husband, was going to float into the room through the window.

I leapt out of bed with the intention of going to my relative's room to sleep when the bedroom door opened and a shaft of electric light from the hall shone into the room and in walked a young girl whom I immediately knew in my mind to be twenty years old. She looked very old-fashioned and wore a long nightdress. Her dark hair, although not very long, was combed back. She neither looked at me nor said a word as she walked past and made towards the bed I had just got out of. I turned my head and said to her, 'It's all right mum, you jump in there because I'm going downstairs to sleep.' I then awoke with the knowledge on my mind that I had seen my mother at the age of twenty.

Three days later Margie came on her usual Monday afternoon visit and whilst chatting I told her about the dream.

'You know why you dreamt that,' she said. 'It was because you have seen the photo of mum when she was twenty.'

I said, 'I don't recall having seen it.'

To which she retorted, 'Oh yes you have because I loaned you several old photographs belonging to mum and dad, and that one was among them.'

I said, 'I do have a vague recollection of you loaning me some photos.'

She then went on to say how a few months earlier she had been talking to our brother Paul about the photo of mum when she was twenty years old, and when Paul said he had never seen it she promised to sort it out and show it to him.

166

She had forgotten her promise until the previous week when she came across the envelope containing the photographs. On Friday evening she took them to Paul's house to show them to him. How ludicrous, I thought, that Margie actually believed it normal for me to have had the dream on the very evening she had chosen to show Paul the photograph when I couldn't even recall having seen it. However, at least I knew Margie to be the one who had influenced my dream. But why, I wondered, did she have cause to think of me that evening? According to my findings one must have cause to think of another before the transmission of thoughts take place, and because I was sleeping at the time I could not have caused the transaction by thinking of her. I asked Margie if she would bring the photographs along on her next visit. This she did the following week. The moment she passed me the envelope containing the photographs I not only understood why she had cause to think of me, but also why she had been so sure I had seen the photograph before. My name and address was on the envelope which meant I had obviously placed them in a used envelope of mine before returning them to her. I took out the photo of mum and saw that instead of a nightdress she was wearing a long skirt and a long-sleeved blouse. Her dark hair was combed back. All very similar to how she had appeared in my dream. Next I studied the envelope and noted it was dated 1977. That was the year my mother died and it was now 1987.

No wonder I couldn't recall having seen the photograph.

It was a short time later that I met one of Kevin's friends and quite naturally Kevin came into our conversation. The lad told me how he and other friends of Kevin's sometimes visit Kevin's grave very late at night and sit around it talking until the early hours of the morning. I asked if they would have done so on the eve of the anniversary of Kevin's death a short time ago. He said they had. This information convinced me that it was they who had influenced my recent dream. I told the lad about the dream I had that night and he looked startled when I began describing the dirty house I found myself in. When I had finished he said, 'So help me, but this is the truth. The house you have just described is the same as the one Kevin went to, and the room is identical to the one he died in'. With these words I suddenly understood so much more

167

about special dreams, and of my recurring dream in which I ever found myself in a strange house where there was always a new room to go into, or discover. (See the report in Chapter 6). I could now understand that the various houses I found myself in were simply the houses of those influencing my dreams, and the room was either the one the person was in at the time, or a particular room they had cause to think about. It was natural for Kevin's friends to think about the house he went to that fatal night. They would then naturally recall the room in which he died. Once they either spoke, or thought of me, all this information was transmitted into the context of my dream.

Hadn't Bill also transmitted details of the new ground floor flat he had purchased, along with concern for the pains in his chest? (Chapter 10).

And was the transmitting of accommodation any different from Kay transmitting into my dream the scene of the countryside where her son had been killed on his motorbike? Because so many of my dreams related to the inside of buildings, I mistakenly placed them in a different category to those that were of the outside. Now I could so easily understand they each came about in exactly the same manner. It is quite possible that Margie either discussed with Paul, or simply recalled in her mind the period of time when she, Winnie and I had slept in the bedroom I found myself in dream 4, and these thoughts, or words played a part in my dream. The similarities between dreams 3 and 4 were simply because dream 3 was still on my mind at the time of having dream 4. I could only marvel at the incredible abilities of the subconscious, and these recent events left me in no doubt that the subconscious does indeed work on a collective basis and that our dreams do not relate to our own lives only. All exactly as my findings implied. I felt quite excited about these recent understandings and wished to know so much more about the strange involvement the subconscious has with the thinking mind.

How, and exactly when, do special dreams come about, I wondered. Something out of the ordinary must trigger them off, otherwise they would be a common feature in life, and why are they so rare?

My findings of 1984 had already implied that the

subconscious made contact with the thinking mind via millions of impulses, and I had already been made aware that whenever I experienced such a dream I was either sleeping in an exhausted state after an extremely hard day's work, or when feeling under the weather. I felt positive my condition did indeed play a role of some importance.

Since nothing works one way only, I reasoned, if the state I am in at the time of experiencing a special dream is significant, then so too must this apply to the one influencing the dream. I had long since understood there to be different kinds of special dreams and those that I believe this theory applied to were those I thought of as *special emotional dreams,* such as dreams 3 and 4 which involved those now departed from this life. Now I began taking into consideration the frame of mind those who had influenced such dreams may well have been in at the time.

Because Margie was very close to my mother she invariably gets a little emotional when discussing her, so I could well imagine her to have been so the evening she spent with Paul showing him the old photographs and the one of mum at the age of twenty.

Two of Kevin's friends had openly wept throughout his funeral service and I am sure they were feeling quite emotional when sitting around his grave late at night.

Even Bill must have been in an extreme state of stress when concerned about the severe pain in his chest. Perhaps he even realized he had but a few months left to live.

Kay was certainly in an emotional state when she spoke of her son who had been killed on his motorbike. She grieved for him throughout her life and hardly one meeting took place that she did not mention his name.

These were just four of the many times I could appreciate that the person influencing my dream would have been either in an emotional state, or one of stress. I believed I had sufficient evidence to support my theory that before a dream of this nature can take place, the one influencing the dream not only has to be in an emotional state, but also have cause to either speak, or think about the person sleeping in an exhausted state. This must take place at precisely the same time before the concerns of the emotional one are transmitted into the context of the sleeper's dream, and it is this information that turns a normal dream into a nightmare. Because the chances of this happening often are pretty remote, it would account for why such dreams are rare.

I made other observations about emotional special dreams, such as the fact that they are dreams, unlike others, they are never forgotten, and in most cases a relative of mine who has now passed away, is either mentioned in the dream, or makes an appearance.

Excluding those nightmares we may have after having watched a horror movie, or those we can easily account for, I believe the nightmares we cannot account for, and which live on in our memory, are those that originate from other people's heartaches, and do not relate to our own lives at all.

Another kind of special dream are those I refer to as *informative special dreams*. These are the dreams that provide me with information about future events. Or those with a message concealed in them like the dream quoted in Chapter 6, in which I found myself looking down on a sunlit market square. I now appreciate that the message being given to me on that occasion was the fact that we communicate without talking. Dreams 1 and 2 were informative dreams since they related to events that were not due to take place in my life until the following day. Some informative dreams, however, relate to incidents that may not take place for several years. Even in dream 2 there was a continuation of the dream a few months later when a rag-and-bone man was blocking the entry to the road of my dream. I believe dreams 1 and 3 came about simply because prior to sleep on each occasion I was thinking about the following day's activities. Before having dream 1 I knew I had to make an early start the following morning and once asleep my subconscious simply continued where my thinking mind had left off. In doing so it included the fact I would be meeting the policeman. Because Thursday was my usual day for going to the Cash & Carry shop it may well be that prior to having dream 2 I was deciding whether or not to go there the following day. Hence my dream. It must be remembered that time as we know it does not exist within the subconscious world.

Whilst studying *informative special dreams* I arrived at another conclusion. I asked myself if dreaming of the policeman and

170

the rag-and-bone man the night before meeting them was any different from when I was dreaming the following day's horse winners. Of course they were not. However, I could understand that because there are *two elements* attached to everything in life, whilst the information supplied to me in dreams 1 and 2 were incidental, the dreaming of the horse winners was intentional on my part. I had unknowingly discovered the correct method of obtaining information from my subconscious. Once again, in accordance with my findings. Next, my mind turned to another kind of special dream. One which did not tally with either of the two already mentioned. These being the one in which I found myself quoting beautiful poetry, and the one in which I was listening to a lecture on medical matters. Neither of which could have originated from my subconscious since I had no knowledge of either subject. The moment I decided to study this kind of dream my mind automatically went to the time John had spoken my thoughts in the midst of holding a conversation. (Chapter 6)

Since my findings were revealed to me in 1984, I have acknowledged the fact that whenever there is something I don't quite understand, or if I am seeking an elusive answer concerning my findings, a past 'event' will immediately appear on my mind as if to say, 'Here is a clue'. It always turns out to be so. On the other hand, should I arrive at a certain conclusion, a past 'event' will still appear on my mind, but one which may prove my conclusion could not possibly be so. I have come to realize that whilst writing this manuscript there are certain occasions when on a particular page I make mistake after mistake, causing me to tear it up and begin over and over again. Finally I came to understand that on each occasion I was missing out important facts on the page concerned. Yet the moment I included them I was able to continue without making one mistake This would indicate to me that we are being directed by the subconscious in all we do.

I re-read the account I had given of John having spoken my thoughts, and when I read the part in which I said, 'I was daydreaming at the time', I had an inner feeling of certainty that this was the clue. I now consider it a possibility that those who influenced the two previously mentioned dreams were actually awake at the time, but were daydreaming whilst either studying, or listening to the subjects involved. This would account for why the dreams had been so direct and did not require a storyline in the same way usual dreams do.

Another understanding I arrived at whilst reading the account of how John had spoken my thoughts, was the fact that I claimed it to be the only occasion such a thing had happened. I could appreciate how wrong this statement had been since John frequently spoke my thoughts, or carried out the same tasks as me, and vice-versa. Our many telephone conversations proved nothing had altered, even when John was living at the coast. The only difference on this occasion was the fact that the thoughts of mine which he spoke were out of keeping with the conversation he was holding at the time. This gave it the appearance of being a freak incident.

I learned so much more about dreams at the time being referred to, but all is too complex for me to include in the writing of this chapter. It is, however, my hope that one day I shall be given the opportunity to discuss everything with those familiar with the subject of dreams.

I would just like to say this: Should anyone believe my story to be mere fabrication, I would consider it to be the greatest compliment ever paid. Only such a superior intelligence as I claim the subconscious to be, is capable of spinning such a complex web to form such an orderly pattern.

15

Apart from the dreaming aspect so much more was going on in my life during the latter part of 1986 and early 1987. Bizarre 'event chains' were in operation in which outrageous coincidences became a regular feature. Yet all took place so casually and down-to-earth. It was during that period I came to understand exactly what a coincidence really is. My dictionary defined the word coincidence as meaning: 'A remarkable occurrence of similar or corresponding events at the same time by chance.' Nothing in life happens by chance. All is part of an intricate pattern created by the unseen world of the collective subconscious whilst in the process of carrying out its purpose in life. The obeying of all our emotional commands, no matter how serious, or how trivial. Only by operating on a collective basis can the individual subconscious accomplish this task.

Now, at the risk of boring you with many seemingly unimportant details concerning my life, I would like to prove this statement. To do so, I must include part of an 'event chain' which was occurring at this time.

One afternoon in early February 1987, I realized that the MOT on a car I owned must be due again. On checking I found it would require one on the 13th February which was just one week away. Because of the car's rust, I knew it would not pass the test, so I decided right then to purchase another car. My special car I had placed in my garage since its repair after the accident.

Although it was raining I decided to post a letter. On the way to the post box I met an elderly couple who were delivering the free newspaper which is sent out each week.. My house being in a different road to the one in which they were delivering the papers, I knew they would not put one through my letterbox so I asked if I may take a copy.

Once back at home I looked in the car advertisements and spotted a car which looked interesting. The advert said one should make enquiries after 6 pm. That evening I rang the owner and he assured me it was a reliable car, and it had a new MOT. I said I would like to view it and perhaps try it out. When he informed me he lived in *an area I was unfamiliar with,* I assured him I would get lost trying to find his house, especially in the dark. He suggested we met half way and asked me to suggest somewhere. I automatically suggested we met *near the church in Dunhill Road.* Because he did not know Dunhill Road I then suggested we made it outside the large *Sainsbury's* store since they stayed open until 8 pm and I could try the car out in their car park. The car was a *red Mini* which I agreed to buy. We made our way to my house where we completed the deal. Because this was a saloon car and not an estate like my old vehicle, I was a little concerned by its lack of space when going to the Cash & Carry shop, but a relative suggested I put the black roof rack on which I had in my garage.

The next day it was reported in our local newspaper that a man in a *red Mini* with a *black roof rack* had tried to pull a young girl into his car *near the church in Dunhill Road.* The following day I was told by the assistant in a newsagent's that he had made a second attempt, but this time had tried to grab a young boy from outside *Sainsbury's.*

The day after purchasing the car I decided to *clear out a drawer* in which I kept paid up bills. As I emptied the contents of the drawer onto the floor I began thinking about *Stella,* an old friend of mine whom I hadn't seen in months. I wondered if she intended *growing plants for my garden again this year.* As I set about destroying old *gas, electric and rates bills* etc, I came across my *missing Central Heating Instructions* which had been required a few weeks earlier. I also found a *Diary* which I had kept for a couple of months during the summer of 1985, for the purpose of recording 'event chains' which were in operation at that time. *Some parts I could not recall having written.* When I read the part concerning *the police I felt very angry* because of the way they had treated a friend of mine at that time, when she had tried to assist them. As I began *recalling the event* in my mind, so my telephone rang. It was a policewoman from our local police station. She asked if I could *recall an incident* which took place just before Christmas 1986. I said I could, and she went on to say how she had just read the *statement* I had made and asked if I would describe the man that had been involved, again. I described the man and then informed her that she could not have been reading the statement I made because I was never asked to make one. Only *Mr Thomas* made a statement. She said she would contact Mr Thomas and come back to me, but she never did.

This took place on the Thursday. On Friday I had an unexpected visit from *Stella*. Her first words were that she had bought the seeds to *grow plants for me again this year.* During the course of our conversation she remarked how fed up she was with the weather and went on to say how the previous day, to amuse herself she had *cleared out a drawer of old gas and electric bills etc.* She then said how she came across her *missing Washing Machine Instructions* and an old *Diary* she had kept years ago. She said how she enjoyed reading it because she *couldn't recall having written most of it.*

As Stella was leaving a young relative of mine called. She told us how her class had been taught how to use a *washing machine* at school that day. The next day was Saturday and whilst out shopping I met *Mr Thomas*. I told him of the call I had received from the police and asked if he had been contacted. He said, 'No' and went on to say, 'don't talk to me about *the police, they make me so angry.* I received a letter from them a few days ago accusing me of leaving the scene of an accident. They said a witness had noted the number of my car and I was to report to the police station and make a *statement.*' He said, 'The accident took place in *an area I never go to.*' He said he went to the police station and was able to prove he was at work on the day in question and that his car was outside his office the whole day. I then told him how I'd bought another car on Wednesday. He said, 'I bought another car on Wednesday too.'

I said, 'Mine is a red one, what colour is yours?'

He said 'Red.' I asked if he'd traded in his old estate car but he said, 'No, I bought the car privately, so still have the estate to get rid of.'

I said, 'Me too.'

These kind of events have been going on throughout my life

175

and such happenings do not occur by chance.

Can you see how each detail on an individual basis is of little importance, yet once connected together, a bizarre pattern emerges. A pattern which covers every aspect of life in such a casual way since it is not meant that we should understand what is taking place. (Then I come along and spoil it all).

Not only do these event chains prove that as we think of another we make subconscious contact and transmit back and forth our thoughts, but our actions also.

Once an emotional command is given, the subconscious automatically sets up a chain of events to form a pattern which may involve many other people whose own emotional desires are also in the process of being dealt with, until perhaps just one event will result in each of their desires being granted at one and the same time. (The intermingling of pieces of puzzle taken from many people's mountain of pieces. Chapter 9.)

Can you understand why I am convinced the many coincidences that take place in life do result from the unseen world of the collective subconscious? Because time is non existent in the subconscious world, the past, present and future are one and the same. Because of this our subconscious mind is aware of future events long before the thinking mind. However, sometimes information about a future event slips through to the conscious mind, thus causing us to include the details made know to us into the context of the conversation we may be holding at the time. This is what took place when I suggested to the man with the car for sale that we met near the church in Dunhill Road, and then altered it to outside Sainsbury's. Not only were they the two places I was due to read about, and hear about in the following two days, but I also suggested each place in the correct order. I feel sure that had the children been approached by the man in the red Mini in two other locations, then they would have been where I'd have suggested our meeting took place.

To prove this point I would like you to carry out a little experiment. The next time you are holding a conversation in your home, make a point of leaving the television on. On many occasions you will hear the very word, or words spoken in your conversation repeated a short time later on the television. On most occasions this will take place almost simultaneously as you speak them. Without having explained the cause, it would be yet another occasion when someone noting the event would have cause to say, 'What a coincidence'.

The next time you make arrangements to meet friends, when the meeting takes place, make a point of asking them about the various conversations and tasks they have carried out since the arrangements were made, and you will find that intermingled among you all, very similar activities have gone on. Should there be something you wished to know prior to the meeting taking place there is a good chance one of your friends will supply you with the answer during the course of the conversation, without having known your need for it. If something out of the ordinary takes place in your life for a second time, make a point of recalling exactly what you were doing the first time it happened, and invariably you will find you were carrying out similar tasks on each occasion. Or look for the many similarities between the two events.

It is my hope to prove that an element of life exists which has gone undetected throughout the ages. Also to prove that anything which takes place on this planet can only have originated from a natural earthly source. Because the many strange events which have been taking place in people's lives throughout the ages, actually came about in the reverse order in which they appeared to the thinking mind, many educated researchers have made little headway in their research programmes. Only because I have been able to conduct my studies on personal experiences, have I been able to succeed where they have failed. Throughout our lives, and on different levels, our subconscious is constantly in the process of setting up these intricate patterns whilst dealing with the flow of emotional commands and requests we make.

In accordance with whether or not we are meant to be present when a crucial last piece of puzzle is about to be laid, so, either Sod's law, or the hand of Providence comes into operation, and each may work for a good cause, or a bad one. To illustrate my meaning, let us assume that someone is eagerly looking forward to a long awaited holiday. Then at the last moment everything goes wrong causing the person to cancel their vacation. This could be blamed on Sod's law. Now, supposing the plane they were due to fly on crashes, and all on board are killed. It could now be claimed that

Providence played a part.

Now a similar situation. A person, desperately in need of a holiday is unexpectedly offered a free one. The hand of Providence. The plane taking the person on holiday crashes, and all on board are killed. We are back to Sod's law.

There is more to this illustration than would appear. Among those who died on the crashed plane another event chain would have been in operation long before the fatal crash took place. An event chain which would have gradually drawn together, all those destined to be on the plane that particular day, for the laying of a final piece of puzzle.

Because Emotions are our means of entry into the unseen world of the subconscious they are exclusive to our daily lives. Emotions do not exist within the subconscious world. Because of this it is vital that the commands we give are clear and precise, not allowing for a bad event to take place before they become reality. The subconscious simply obeys regardless of the consequences. It was for this reason I said in Chapter 13, 'Once fully understood my findings of the truth are a hundred times more alarming than the creepiest of ghost stories, When everyone realizes that every emotional thought, or great desire, good or bad, that you may have in the private world of your thinking mind affects all those around you, only then will you understand the full importance of all I am trying to reveal.' I believe every accident, or tragedy, that takes place in life results purely from badly worded commands having been given, or by fearing a certain tragic event will take place. Because of all that has taken place in my life I had no doubts whatsoever that it is via our emotions that we communicate with the subconscious world, and it is via millions of impulses and inspirational thoughts that the subconscious is able to make contact with the thinking mind in order to respond to our desires.

I could even appreciate that without those involved in the many 'event chains' having responded to such impulses, the bizarre patterns could not have formed. Yet I still felt there was an important factor which had not yet been made known to me, but what I had no idea.

It was a month or two later, at a time when I was deeply involved with daily tasks when for no apparent reason a new thought flashed across my mind. One that said, 'Not just

178

IMPULSES & INSPIRATIONAL THOUGHTS, but MAGNETICALLY CHARGED IMPULSES & INSPIRA-TIONAL THOUGHTS'. Immediately I recalled my experience where I found myself looking down on the earth from a great height and realizing I was looking down on a magnificent electrical system, (Chapter 13), and my new thoughts fitted in so perfectly. I also recalled how in the report described in Chapter 6 I was quoted as saying, 'It's as though, out in space there is a MASS I can tune in to'. I now believe that mass exists here on earth and is none other than the magnetic field created by the collective subconscious. I concluded, that whilst our emotional commands together with utter belief in our convictions link us to the subconscious world, it is via magnetically charged impulses and inspirations that the subconscious makes contact into our daily lives, and it is via this process that we are able to determine the destiny of our own lives. I could appreciate also, that because every word and everything in life has a counterpart, this enables us to have a choice in all we do in life. Without this choice we could not determine our own destiny.

Because counterparts are the means by which we are able to determine our own destiny, these too are exclusive to the conscious mind. This being so would indicate that good or evil exists in man's thinking mind which would indeed make man responsible for everything that takes place on earth. The good and bad alike. This idea I found more acceptable than the religion I was taught as a child, in which it claimed man to be responsible for the bad things that happened, and gave God credit for the good. Nothing in life works one way only. Because the individual subconscious, quite naturally, can only respond to one thinking mind, all our emotional commands and desires, good or bad, and regardless to whom they were originally directed, must eventually take place in our own lives. However, because there are many ways by which our desires may be granted, and our deeds repaid, and because many years may pass before it is appropriate for the subconscious to respond to various commands given, we fail to associate the happenings in our lives with our own past actions, thoughts and desires. The repayment of our deeds is but an automatic function. How true the saying, 'When you dig a hole for someone, be sure to dig one for yourself.'

Because there are varying degrees of emotions this enables each of our commands to be obeyed, even those of a very minor nature. It also enables a strong emotional plea for forgiveness to override a command already in the process of being repeated in the life of a wrongdoer. Therefore even forgiveness by the subconscious is possible.

Unfortunately, in life, whilst we are able to forgive others the wrong they do, we sometimes find it impossible to forgive ourselves. A plea for forgiveness is one of the rare occasions when the subconscious is instructed in the correct manner, since we know the wrong we have done and express it precisely in our prayers when asking forgiveness. Prayers are of the utmost importance since regardless of whether they are directed at a religion of our choice, or even at a totem pole, they are still intercepted by the subconscious.

I liken our emotions to a bunch of keys which will each unlock the same door. In the same way we are only able to use one key at a time, so too are we able to experience only one emotion at a time. We may, of course, alternate from one emotion to another in quick succession, such as from anger to frustration, but we never experience the two at precisely the same time. Because the various emotions we experience arise from circumstances and situations, no matter how hard we try, we can never experience an emotion at will. Because of this we shall never be able to control the subconscious. But we are able to control our thoughts, while we experience our emotion, and it is my belief that it is vital we learn to do so. It would appear that not only has everything in life a counterpart, but a double purpose also. I believe this to be true of the subconscious mind. Not only are we able to determine our own destiny via the subconscious, but I believe it to be the source from where all learning and knowledge is acquired.

Now, instead of the subconscious being the servant and the conscious mind the master, the subconscious becomes the teacher, and the conscious mind the pupil. Not only would it appear that man had been provided with the materials to improve his daily existence, but the blueprints also. Each he had first to discover. The thinking mind has only the power to reason and discover, and only that which already exists may be discovered.

I believe, whilst the many inventions created by man represents a natural element of life which is visible to the eye, the many technical devices man has introduced into our daily lives in the form of transmitters, receivers, radar, projectors, screens, television etc, are but imitations of either the subconscious, or the conscious mind's natural abilities, and the principle of the computer is based on the subconscious mind itself. The subconscious being the most supreme computer ever devised. I also believe, in the same way that a manmade computer is unable to relate to time, emotions, the different sexes and counterparts, this is also true of the collective magnetic world of the subconscious and these are important facts to remember when trying to understand this 'higher form of intelligence' which arises from the human brain.

Because everything in life has a counterpart this creates a dividing line which equally halves everything pertaining to life on this planet. Yet each half is vital to the other. How could there be night without day, sun without rain, food without water, good without evil, wrong without right, love without hate, negative without positive, man without woman, or even life without death?

I believe two forms of life do originate from the human brain. The subconscious and its counterpart, the conscious mind. Since everything in life has a counterpart, this must be true of life also. Is it really too incredible to believe that the unseen qualities of life originate from a natural earthly source?

16

For the past four years or so I have been gathering evidence to support my belief, that from within the workings of the subconscious world, a numerical system is in operation which influences our lives in a most complex fashion. A numerical system which enables the subconscious world to segregate those, who by fear, or accidentally, destined themselves to be present during the laying of a final piece of puzzle. A numerical system of which number 9 is the most important of all numbers.

These more recent findings came about as a result of desperately wishing to know why certain dates of the year, together with just four numbers, 9, 11, 14 and 25 appeared to have played a vital role in my life.

Prior to my findings having been revealed to me in 1984, I had already acquired a vague kind of inner awareness that number 9 was the most important of the four numbers, whilst 11 and 14 were of equal value. 25 I considered to be a whole, or complete number since it made an appearance only on a rare special occasion. The three dates concerned, these being the 14th February, 11th June and the 29th June appeared to correspond with 11 and 14 since even 29 when added together equals 11. I had considered it a possibility that the fact I was born on the 25th of the 11th month had some bearing as to why these particular numbers should be ever present in my life, since $25 - 11 = 14$, and by adding $25 + 11$ across it equals 9. The very same four numbers. However, this was only surmise. Whilst I am not prepared at this time, to provide a long drawn-out account of how I arrived at the above mentioned conclusion, or all that I discovered, I hope to include in this chapter sufficient evidence to support my claim, and leave it to you, the reader, to decide if my claims appear to be so, or that all amounts to nothing more than a fluke.

These findings relate only to those deaths that come about via unnatural causes. It would appear that when death occurs via accidental means, or intentionally, one or the other of four elements are always present. Sometimes more than one. I will now reveal just three of the four elements.

Remember the numbers I refer to will be 9, 11, 14 and on the rare occasion 25.

ELEMENT ONE

Of the 365 days there are in each year, 72 of them are days on which a tragic loss of life by unnatural means is likely to occur. (73 in a leap year).

The days of the month that I refer to as risky days are the 9th, 11th, 14th, 18th, 27th and the 29th.

365 days in a year,	3 + 6 + 5 =	14
72 risky days,	=	9
293 safe days,	=	14

These findings account for the date element.

ELEMENT TWO

Basing life expectancy on 100 years, there are 25 ages when a person is most likely to become the victim of death by unnatural means, or the age of the one causing a tragic loss of life, either accidentally, or intentionally.

The 25 ages are as follows:

1	2	3	4	5	6	7	8	(9)	10
(11)	12	13	(14)	15	16	17	(18)	19	20
21	22	23	24	25	26	(27)	28	(29)	30
31	32	33	34	35	(36)	37	(38)	39	40
41	42	43	44	(45)	46	(47)	48	49	50
51	52	53	(54)	55	(56)	57	58	(59)	60
61	62	(63)	64	(65)	66	67	(68)	69	70
71	(72)	73	(74)	75	76	(77)	78	79	80
(81)	82	(83)	84	85	(86)	87	88	89	(90)
91	(92)	93	94	(95)	96	97	98	99	100

These being each of the numbers which are equivalent to 9, 11 or 14.

Note how in the above diagram yet another pattern has formed.

Three diagonal lines, and the segregation of numbers 9 at the bottom of the chart, and 11 and 14 at the top.

Even the fact there are 4 elements to relate to 4 numbers may also be of some significance since there are 4 seasons in each year, and 4 directions, north, south, east and west. Plus every 4th year is a leap year.

ELEMENT THREE

Element three usually appears on the scene when a major tragedy takes place in which many lives are lost. Even so, element one or element two may also be present.

Element three consists of the adding across the total number of people killed in the disaster.

I will now list, as briefly as possible, many of the tragic events I believe fit into this category, followed by major tragic events which relate to element one.

THE TITANIC
1,523 lives were lost, 1 + 5 + 2 + 3 = 11   = 11

THE EMPRESS OF IRELAND
1,062 people lost their lives,   = 9

HMS ROYAL OAK
810 men lost their lives,   = 9

THE ABERFAN DISASTER
144 lives were lost,   = 9

THE BRADFORD STADIUM FOOTBALL
DISASTER
56 people lost their lives,   = 11

THE EDINBURGH POPPY DAY SERVICE
MASSACRE
11 people were killed,   = 11

THE GREEK FERRY MASSACRE
9 people were killed,   = 9

NEW YORK SCHOOL BUS TRAGEDY
27 teenagers died in blazing bus,   = 9

BOEING 707 AIRLINER WHICH CRASHED
IN THE AZORES
144 people lost their lives,   = 9

THE HILLSBOROUGH FOOTBALL STADIUM
TRAGEDY
95 lives were lost,   = 14

THE PIPER ALPHA OIL RIG TRAGEDY
167 men lost their lives,   = 14

THE RANSTEIN AIR SHOW TRAGEDY
45 lives were lost,   = 9

THE MANCHESTER AIR CRASH
54 people died of smoke inhalation,   = 9

FEBRUARY 1989
9 people were sucked out of a Jumbo Jet
   flying at 22,000ft,   = 9

EXPLOSION ON BOARD AN AMERICAN
WARSHIP IN THE ATLANTIC
47 men lost their lives,   = 11

M1 AIR CRASH
47 people died,   = 11

DC-10 BLOWN OUT OF THE SKY
IN THE SAHARA
171 on board, no survivors found,   = 9

3/6/1990
11 British holiday makers abroad, died
   in speeding bus   = 11

THE IRANIAN AIR BUS ACCIDENTALLY
SHOT DOWN BY THE AMERICANS
270 people lost their lives,   = 9

THE LOCKERBIE AIR DISASTER
270 people also lost their lives,   = 9

Could it really be classed as a coincidence that the same number of people lost their lives in both the Iranian Air Bus tragedy, and the Lockerbie disaster when it is believed the Lockerbie disaster to have been an act of retaliation for the shooting down of the Iranian Air Bus?

Next I will give account of major tragedies in which element one was present. A few, you will notice, are also related to element three. Maybe they all do, but because I have no account of the lives lost in the following tragic events, I cannot say.

THE TITANIC
Went down on the   14th February

THE EMPRESS OF IRELAND
Sank on the   29th May

THE ASCOT
Went down on the   29th March

THE NANCY MOLLER
Went down on the   18th March

THE DAISY MOLLER
Went down on the   14th February

THE BEHAR
Went down on the   9th March

HMS ROYAL OAK
Went down on the   14th October

HMS ARK ROYAL
Went down on the   14th November

HMS BARHAM (almost my surname)
Went down on the (my birthday)   25th November

THE VALENTINE MASSACRE
Took place on the   14th February

THE KINGS CROSS TRAGEDY
Took place on the   18th November

I wondered if it were possible the system would have been
in operation during the war years when chaos reigned. I could
recall just six tragic events of which I was sure of the details.
Each of the six tragic events collaborated with either element
two, three or four.

Quite recently I came across the April edition of a 1981

newspaper in which I read the following:

> *On that fateful date – November 25, 1944 – a war-time rumour had drawn many shoppers to Woolworths on the Saturday when a German rocket (V2) crashed down killing 164 people and injuring hundreds. This took place in New Cross Road which was then in the Borough of Deptford.*

This tragic event relates to element three since 164 people were killed. It was also one of the rare occasions 25 made an appearance.

I now believe my assumption about numbers 9, 11, 14 and 25 to be correct, except that number 9 is not just the most important of the four numbers, but the most important of all numbers.

I made other observations about number 9, such as the fact that a pregnancy lasts for 9 months. Could it be, I wondered, that number 9 relates to birth and death?

Other observations were that there are 9 planets in our Solar System, and just 9 numbers in our numerical system, plus 0 which although not a number, is as vital as the Sun is to the Earth.

Should my belief that a numerical system is in operation be proved authentic, this would suggest to me that man has quite unknowingly penetrated the unseen world of the collective magnetic subconscious, and re-created into our daily lives a numerical system which has obviously been in operation since life first appeared on the earth. Therefore, verifying my statement that only that which already exists may be discovered.

Because my findings offer me a logical answer for every query I have ever had about life, regardless of what is written in books, or believed by educated scholars, I now have my own concept of life on this planet, and how it all came about. A theory which I find wholly acceptable. Because I cannot believe anything so intricate, yet so perfect could just happen. To believe such a thing I would also have to believe that should I throw 500 pieces of a jigsaw puzzle into the air, it would be possible for them to correctly interlock before reaching the ground. Therefore, I must indeed believe there to be a creator of this magnificent creation.

However, I do not believe it to be one who plays any part whatsoever during our time on earth, but one who, having created this magnificent set up, programmed it to provide the family of man with everything that would ever be required throughout the cycle of time during which life is destined to exist on the earth. Because everything pertaining to life results from a chain reaction, I believe only the beginning of time required programming. I believe, in the beginning, from the early elements there came seeds that vegetated the earth. Followed by seeds of life of many descriptions. Some species, having served their purpose, gradually became extinct, whilst new forms of life were still appearing. Among them the human species. A process which took place over the course of millions of years. I believe the first generation of human life was raised by the animals, but mankind having been created superior to all creatures by having been given the thinking mind with which to reason, segregated from the animal kingdom and set about exploring his surroundings and improving his existence. I believe that even the appearance of human life was a slow process, which took place over the course of thousands of years in various parts of the world. This would account for early civilizations.

I believe, that from every living creature there arose a magnetic substance, a guiding force, without which no form of life could have survived past the first generation. A magnetic attracting or repelling action which enabled each to communicate with its own species only. Thus keeping segregated the various species. A guiding force which directed each species in its own particular breeding habit, and directed each in carrying out its purpose in life. Therefore, incorporating all forms of life in the magnetic world. I believe that vegetation responds to the magnetism from within the earth, and the earth to the magnetic universe.

It is my belief that man, having been given the thinking mind with which to reason, was set the task of discovering all that nature bestowed, and all life's secrets. Yet even whilst in the progress of discovering and learning, man was also destined to be in the process of destroying, first the natural elements and finally, all forms of life also (Life's double purpose). Following such destruction, I believe, the earth will then lie fallow for millions of years recuperating its natural resources, until such time as new seeds are ready to be sown, and another cycle will begin all over again. Only when death on earth takes place will we understand why.

Everything that has ever taken place in my life, no matter how seemingly bizarre, did in fact come about in an extremely down-to-earth fashion. I did not see visions, or hear voices. When I spoke of my Invisible Teacher I was simply referring to my subconscious. In spite of my one true belief having always been in 'the power of the human brain', because of age-old misguided beliefs which have been passed down through the generations, that all unseen elements of life originate from either a religious source, an evil one, from outer space, or as spiritualists would have us believe, from the next world, throughout my search for the truth I never strayed too far from one or the other of these convictions.

It was my new exciting 'compulsive thoughts' that in one clean sweep brushed all these myths aside and revealed the true source from which everything originates. That is the collective magnetic subconscious which I believe represents a form of life in its own right.

Because my findings relate closely to the religion I was taught as a child, I can appreciate that occultism and forms of religion, which exist in the world are each based on the truth of my findings. It is man's interpretation of this truth, together with age-old beliefs, rituals, and customs which man has allowed to evolve around each interpretation, which is the cause of so much conflict and bloodshed.

I believe the magnetic subconscious represents a universal religion which is in operation throughout our lives, automatically repaying our deeds, and regardless of our daily beliefs. A UNIVERSAL RELIGION which must be observed by all.